California DMV Exam Workbook:

Your Essential Guide to the California Driving Test

Master the California DMV Exam with the Best California Driver's Practice Tests

Introduction

Driving is a crucial aspect of daily life in California, and navigating the roads safely and confidently is essential for both new and experienced drivers. If you are preparing to take your California driving test, you are likely feeling a mix of excitement and nerves. You may wonder what to expect on the test and how to prepare best to pass it on the first try.

In this book, we provide you with everything you need to know about the California practice driving test. We will cover the different types of driving tests offered in California, the process for obtaining a driver's license, and the requirements you must meet to be eligible for a license.

We will also delve into the rules of the road and safety measures you should be aware of as a driver in California.

We understand that preparing for the driving test can be stressful, so we have included a wealth of information and resources to help you feel more confident and prepared on test day. We will provide tips and strategies for improving your driving skills and increasing your chances of passing the test.

We will also provide practice test questions and sample scenarios to better understand what to expect on the test.

But the goal of this book is not just to help you pass the driving test. Our ultimate aim is to help you become a responsible and safe driver. Driving is a privilege that comes with great responsibility, and we want to empower you with the knowledge and skills necessary to navigate the roads confidently and with care.

So whether you are a first-time driver looking to obtain your license or an experienced driver seeking to refresh your knowledge of California driving laws, this book is for you. We hope it serves as a valuable resource as you prepare for your driving test and embark on your journey as a licensed driver in California.

Table of Contents

Vehicle equipment and maintenance 81

This includes knowledge of the various parts of a vehicle and how to properly maintain them, as well as knowledge of how to safely load and unload a vehicle.

Sharing the road 109

This includes information about how to safely share the road with other vehicles, pedestrians, and bicycles.

This includes knowledge of the rules and regulations surrounding the transportation of hazardous materials by commercial vehicles.

This includes information about the requirements for registering and insuring a vehicle in California.

This includes knowledge of how to handle various types of emergencies that may occur while driving, such as blowouts, fires, and collisions.

Vehicle size and weight limits

This includes knowledge of the size and weight limits for vehicles on California roads, as well as the rules for towing.

Public transportation

This includes information about the various types of public transportation available in California, as well as the rules for using them.

Traffic laws and signs

In this chapter on traffic laws and signs, you will find a variety of questions and answers designed to help you understand and learn the important rules and regulations of driving in California. These questions and answers will cover a wide range of topics, including traffic laws, traffic signs, and traffic signals.

By working through these questions and answers, you will have the opportunity to test your knowledge and identify areas where you may need further study. It is important to thoroughly review and understand the material in this chapter, as a strong understanding of traffic laws and signs is crucial for safe and responsible driving.

Welcome to the practice exam on traffic laws and signs! In this exam, you will be tested on your knowledge of California's traffic laws and your ability to interpret and follow traffic signs and signals. There will be a total of 15 questions, and you will need to answer at least 12 to pass correctly.

We encourage you to thoroughly review and study the relevant materials before attempting the exam. This practice exam is a great opportunity to test your knowledge and identify areas where you may need further study.

After you have completed the exam, the answers will be provided so that you can check your work and see how you did. Remember, this is a practice exam, so don't worry if you don't get every question right.

For training purposes, you can mark the ☐ symbol next to what you think is the correct answer: Once you have chosen the correct answer, use a pencil or pen to mark the ☐ symbol next to that answer.

You can become proficient in traffic laws and signs with dedication and hard work and be well-prepared for your California driving test. Good luck!

Traffic laws and signs exam

1. **What should you do when you come to a stop sign?**

   A. ☐ Slow down and proceed with caution

   B. ☐ Come to a complete stop, then proceed when safe

   C. ☐ Honk your horn to let other drivers know you are there

   D. ☐ Drive through the stop sign without stopping

2. **What does a flashing red traffic light mean?**

   A. ☐ Stop and wait for the light to turn green

   B. ☐ Slow down and proceed with caution

   C. ☐ Stop only if there is cross traffic

   D. ☐ Yield to pedestrians

3. **What should you do when you see a pedestrian in a crosswalk?**

   A. ☐ Speed up to get through the crosswalk before the pedestrian

   B. ☐ Stop and wait for the pedestrian to cross

   C. ☐ Honk your horn to let the pedestrian know you are there

   D. ☐ Proceed with caution and be prepared to stop if necessary

4.   **What does a yellow diamond-shaped sign with a black X on it mean?**

    A. ☐ No passing

    B. ☐ Yield

    C. ☐ Stop

    D. ☐ Do not enter

5.   **What should you do when you see a school bus with its red lights flashing and a stop sign extended?**

    A. ☐ Slow down and proceed with caution

    B. ☐ Stop at least 20 feet away from the bus

    C. ☐ Pass the bus on the right side

    D. ☐ Continue driving because the bus is not on your side of the road

6.   **When driving at night, what should you do if you are approaching a vehicle from behind with its high beams on?**

    A. ☐ Flash your high beams to let the other driver know their high beams are on

    B. ☐ Turn your high beams on to improve your visibility

    C. ☐ Turn your low beams off to avoid dazzling the other driver

    D. ☐ Honk your horn to alert the other driver

7.   **What should you do when you see a yield sign?**

    A. ☐ Stop and wait for all other traffic to go first
    B. ☐ Slow down and proceed with caution, yielding to other vehicles and pedestrians as necessary
    C. ☐ Proceed at the same speed as other traffic
    D. ☐ Increase your speed to get through the intersection before other traffic

8.   **What does a red triangle with an exclamation point on a yellow background mean?**

    A. ☐ Yield
    B. ☐ Stop
    C. ☐ Warning
    D. ☐ Do not enter

9.   **What does a white rectangle with a red border and the letters "RR" on it mean?**

    A. ☐ Stop
    B. ☐ Yield
    C. ☐ Railroad crossing
    D. ☐ No passing

10. **When driving on the road with a single solid white line on your side of the road, you must:**

    A. ☐ Stay in your lane at all times

    B. ☐ Cross the line to pass slower vehicles

    C. ☐ Follow the line as a guide for your position on the road

    D. ☐ Ignore the line and drive as you see fit

11. **What should you do when you see a pedestrian using a white cane or guide dog?**

    A. ☐ Stop and wait for the pedestrian to cross

    B. ☐ Proceed with caution and be prepared to stop if necessary

    C. ☐ Honk your horn to let the pedestrian know you are there

    D. ☐ Speed up to get through the crosswalk before the pedestrian

12. **What does a red octagon with the word "STOP" on it mean?**

    A. ☐ Yield

    B. ☐ Stop

    C. ☐ Warning

    D. ☐ Do not enter

13. **What does a yellow diamond-shaped sign with a black person on it mean?**

   A. ☐ Pedestrian crossing
   B. ☐ School zone
   C. ☐ No passing
   D. ☐ Yield

14. **What does a white rectangle with a green border and the letters "EXIT" on it mean?**

   A. ☐ Exit
   B. ☐ Yield
   C. ☐ Stop
   D. ☐ Do not enter

15. **When driving in a business or residential area, what is the minimum distance you must stop behind a school bus when its red lights are flashing and the stop sign is extended?**

   A. ☐ 10 feet
   B. ☐ 20 feet
   C. ☐ 30 feet
   D. ☐ 50 feet

Correct answers for traffic laws and signs exam

1. **B.** Come to a complete stop, then proceed when safe

2. **A.** Stop and wait for the light to turn green

3. **B.** Stop and wait for the pedestrian to cross

4. **A.** No passing

5. **B.** Stop at least 20 feet away from the bus

6. **C.** Turn your low beams off to avoid dazzling the other driver

7. **B.** Slow down and proceed with caution, yielding to other vehicles and pedestrians as necessary

8. **C.** Warning

9. **C.** Railroad crossing

10. **A.** Stay in your lane at all times

11. **A.** Stop and wait for the pedestrian to cross

12. **B.** Stop

13. **A.** Pedestrian crossing

14. **A.** Exit

15. **B.** 20 feet

Traffic laws and signs exam 2

1. **What should you do when you see a flashing yellow light at an intersection?**

   A. ☐ Stop and wait for the light to turn green

   B. ☐ Proceed with caution and be prepared to stop if necessary

   C. ☐ Yield to pedestrians and other vehicles

   D. ☐ Increase your speed to get through the intersection before other traffic

2. **What does a white rectangle with a red border and the letters "ST" on it mean?**

   A. ☐ Stop

   B. ☐ Yield

   C. ☐ School zone

   D. ☐ No passing

3. **What does a red circle with a white X on it mean?**

   A. ☐ Stop

   B. ☐ Yield

   C. ☐ Warning

   D. ☐ Do not enter

4. **If you see a yield sign while driving, you must:**

   A. ☐ Stop and wait for all other vehicles to pass

   B. ☐ Slow down and be prepared to stop if necessary

   C. ☐ Proceed with caution and give the right-of-way to oncoming traffic

   D. ☐ Ignore the sign and continue driving as usual

5.   **What should you do when you come to a yield sign at an intersection?**

   A. ☐ Stop and wait for all other traffic to go first
   B. ☐ Slow down and proceed with caution, yielding to other vehicles and pedestrians as necessary
   C. ☐ Proceed at the same speed as other traffic
   D. ☐ Increase your speed to get through the intersection before other traffic

6.   **What does a yellow diamond-shaped sign with a black downward-pointing arrow on it mean?**

   A. ☐ No passing
   B. ☐ Yield
   C. ☐ Stop
   D. ☐ Do not enter

7.   **What does a white rectangle with a red border and the letters "HOSP" on it mean?**

   A. ☐ Hospital
   B. ☐ Yield
   C. ☐ Stop
   D. ☐ Do not enter

8.   **What does a yellow triangle with an exclamation point on it mean?**

   A. ☐ Yield
   B. ☐ Stop
   C. ☐ Warning
   D. ☐ Do not enter

9.   **What should you do when you see a school bus with its red lights flashing and a stop sign extended on the other side of a divided highway?**

    A. ☐ Slow down and proceed with caution

    B. ☐ Stop at least 20 feet away from the bus

    C. ☐ Pass the bus on the right side

    D. ☐ Continue driving because the bus is not on your side of the road

10.   **What does a white rectangle with a green border and the letters "ENTER" on it mean?**

    A. ☐ Enter

    B. ☐ Yield

    C. ☐ Stop

    D. ☐ Do not enter

11.   **What should you do when you see a pedestrian using a white cane or guide dog at a crosswalk?**

    A. ☐ Stop and wait for the pedestrian to cross

    B. ☐ Proceed with caution and be prepared to stop if necessary

    C. ☐ Honk your horn to let the pedestrian know you are there

    D. ☐ Speed up to get through the crosswalk before the pedestrian

12.   **What does a yellow diamond-shaped sign with a black left-pointing arrow on it mean?**

    A. ☐ No passing

    B. ☐ Yield

    C. ☐ Stop

    D. ☐ Turn left only

13. **At a four-way stop intersection, who has the right-of-way?**

   A. ☐ The first car to arrive at the intersection
   B. ☐ The car on the right
   C. ☐ The car on the left
   D. ☐ The car going straight

14. **What does a white rectangle with a green border and the letters "PARK" on it mean?**

   A. ☐ Parking area
   B. ☐ Yield
   C. ☐ Stop
   D. ☐ Do not enter

15. **When driving in a residential area, what is the maximum speed limit unless otherwise posted?**

   A. ☐ 35 mph
   B. ☐ 25 mph
   C. ☐ 45 mph
   D. ☐ 55 mph

Correct answers to traffic laws and signs exam 2

1. **B.** Proceed with caution and be prepared to stop if necessary
2. **C.** School zone
3. **A.** Stop
4. **C.** Proceed with caution and give the right-of-way to oncoming traffic
5. **B.** Slow down and proceed with caution, yielding to other vehicles and pedestrians as necessary
6. **D.** Do not enter
7. **A.** Hospital
8. **C.** Warning
9. **D.** Continue driving because the bus is not on your side of the road
10. **A.** Enter
11. **A.** Stop and wait for the pedestrian to cross
12. **D.** Turn left only
13. **A.** The first car to arrive at the intersection
14. **A.** Parking area
15. **B.** 25 mph

Traffic laws and signs exam 3

1.   **What should you do when you come to an intersection with a traffic light that is not working?**

   A. ☐ Treat it as a four-way stop
   B. ☐ Proceed with caution and treat it as a yield sign
   C. ☐ Ignore the intersection and continue driving
   D. ☐ Wait for another driver to go first

2.   **What does a white rectangle with a red border and the letters "WRONG WAY" on it mean?**

   A. ☐ Wrong way
   B. ☐ Yield
   C. ☐ Stop
   D. ☐ Do not enter

3.   **What does a red circle with a white line through it mean?**

   A. ☐ Stop
   B. ☐ Yield
   C. ☐ Warning
   D. ☐ Do not enter

4.   **What should you do when you see a pedestrian in an unmarked crosswalk?**

   A. ☐ Stop and wait for the pedestrian to cross
   B. ☐ Proceed with caution and be prepared to stop if necessary
   C. ☐ Honk your horn to let the pedestrian know you are there
   D. ☐ Speed up to get through the crosswalk before the pedestrian

5.   **What does a yellow diamond-shaped sign with a black right-pointing arrow on it mean?**

   A. ☐ No passing

   B. ☐ Yield

   C. ☐ Stop

   D. ☐ Turn right only

6.   **What does a white rectangle with a red border and the letters "STOP AHEAD" on it mean?**

   A. ☐ Stop ahead

   B. ☐ Yield

   C. ☐ Stop

   D. ☐ Do not enter

7.   **What do a white rectangle with a green border and the letters "INFO" on it mean?**

   A. ☐ Information

   B. ☐ Yield

   C. ☐ Stop

   D. ☐ Do not enter

8.   **What should you do when you see a school bus with its red lights flashing and a stop sign extended on your side of a divided highway?**

   A. ☐ Slow down and proceed with caution

   B. ☐ Stop at least 20 feet away from the bus

   C. ☐ Pass the bus on the right side

   D. ☐ Continue driving because the bus is not on your side of the road

9.   **What does a yellow triangle with a black person on it mean?**

   A. ☐ Pedestrian crossing

   B. ☐ School zone

   C. ☐ Yield

   D. ☐ Do not enter

10.   **What should you do when you see a pedestrian using a white cane or guide dog at an intersection?**

   A. ☐ Stop and wait for the pedestrian to cross

   B. ☐ Proceed with caution and be prepared to stop if necessary

   C. ☐ Honk your horn to let the pedestrian know you are there

   D. ☐ Speed up to get through the intersection before the pedestrian

11.   **What does a white rectangle with a green border and the letters "EXIT" on it mean?**

   A. ☐ Exit

   B. ☐ Yield

   C. ☐ Stop

   D. ☐ Do not enter

12.   **What should you do when you come to a stop sign at an intersection?**

   A. ☐ Slow down and proceed with caution

   B. ☐ Come to a complete stop, then proceed when safe

   C. ☐ Honk your horn to let other drivers know you are there

   D. ☐ Drive through the stop sign without stopping

13. **What does a yellow diamond-shaped sign with a black left-pointing arrow and a black right-pointing arrow on it mean?**

   A. ☐ No passing

   B. ☐ Yield

   C. ☐ Stop

   D. ☐ Turn left or right only

14. **What does a white rectangle with a red border and the letters "RRX" on it mean?**

   A. ☐ Stop

   B. ☐ Yield

   C. ☐ Railroad crossing ahead

   D. ☐ No passing

15. **What should you do when you see a pedestrian in a marked crosswalk?**

   A. ☐ Stop and wait for the pedestrian to cross

   B. ☐ Proceed with caution and be prepared to stop if necessary

   C. ☐ Honk your horn to let the pedestrian know you are there

   D. ☐ Speed up to get through the crosswalk before the pedestrian

Correct answers for traffic laws and signs exam 3

1. **A.** Treat it as a four-way stop
2. **A.** Wrong way
3. **D.** Do not enter
4. **B.** Proceed with caution and be prepared to stop if necessary
5. **D.** Turn right only
6. **A.** Stop ahead
7. **A.** Information
8. **B.** Stop at least 20 feet away from the bus
9. **A.** Pedestrian crossing
10. **A.** Stop and wait for the pedestrian to cross
11. **A.** Exit
12. **B.** Come to a complete stop, then proceed when safe
13. **D.** Turn left or right only
14. **C.** Railroad crossing ahead
15. **A.** Stop and wait for the pedestrian to cross

Traffic laws and signs exam 4

1. **What does a YIELD sign indicate?**

   A. ☐ Stop completely before proceeding

   B. ☐ Slow down and proceed with caution

   C. ☐ Proceed with the right-of-way

   D. ☐ Stop and wait for a green light

2. **When driving at night, you must use your headlights when visibility is:**

   A. ☐ Less than 500 feet

   B. ☐ Less than 1,000 feet

   C. ☐ Less than 1,500 feet

   D. ☐ Less than 2,000 feet

3. **What is the correct hand signal for a right turn?**

   A. ☐ Arm extended straight up

   B. ☐ Arm extended straight out

   C. ☐ Arm extended straight down

   D. ☐ Arm extended horizontally

4. **When approaching a school bus with flashing red lights, you must:**

   A. ☐ Slow down and proceed with caution

   B. ☐ Stop and wait for the bus to move on

   C. ☐ Proceed with the right-of-way

   D. ☐ Increase your speed to pass the bus quickly

5. What is the minimum distance you must leave between your vehicle and a pedestrian crossing the road in a marked crosswalk?

A. ☐ 3 feet

B. ☐ 5 feet

C. ☐ 7 feet

D. ☐ 10 feet

6. When driving on a multi-lane road, you may only pass another vehicle on the left if:

A. ☐ There are no vehicles in the right lane

B. ☐ The vehicle in the left lane is turning right

C. ☐ The vehicle in the right lane is turning left

D. ☐ It is safe to do so and there is a broken white line separating the lanes

7. When driving in fog, you should use your:

A. ☐ High beams

B. ☐ Low beams

C. ☐ Fog lights

D. ☐ Hazard lights

8. What is the speed limit in a school zone when children are present and the lights are flashing?

A. ☐ 15 mph

B. ☐ 20 mph

C. ☐ 25 mph

D. ☐ 30 mph

9. When you see a pedestrian using a white cane or a service animal, you must:

A. ☐ Yield the right-of-way

B. ☐ Proceed with caution

C. ☐ Stop and wait for the pedestrian to cross

D. ☐ Honk your horn to alert the pedestrian

10. When approaching a four-way stop, who has the right of way?

A. ☐ The first vehicle to arrive

B. ☐ The vehicle on the right

C. ☐ The vehicle on the left

D. ☐ The vehicle going straight

11. When you see a flashing red light at a railroad crossing, you must:

A. ☐ Stop and wait for the train to pass

B. ☐ Proceed with caution

C. ☐ Yield the right-of-way to the train

D. ☐ Increase your speed to pass the train quickly

12. What is the correct hand signal for a left turn?

A. ☐ Arm extended straight up

B. ☐ Arm extended straight out

C. ☐ Arm extended straight down

D. ☐ Arm extended horizontally

13. When driving on a two-way road, you must drive on the:

A. ☐ The left side of the road

B. ☐ The right side of the road

C. ☐ Center of the road

D. ☐ Shoulder of the road

14. If you are driving on the road with two lanes in each direction and you want to change lanes, you should:

A. ☐ Signal your intention and change lanes slowly

B. ☐ Signal your intention and change lanes quickly

C. ☐ Do not signal and change lanes quickly

D. ☐ Do not signal and change lanes slowly

15. What is the minimum distance you must leave between your vehicle and a bicycle when passing in the same lane?

A. ☐ 3 feet

B. ☐ 5 feet

C. ☐ 7 feet

D. ☐ 10 feet

Correct answers for traffic laws and signs exam 4

1. **B.** Slow down and proceed with caution
2. **A.** Less than 500 feet
3. **B.** Arm extended straight out
4. **B.** Stop and wait for the bus to move on
5. **A.** 3 feet
6. **D.** It is safe to do so and there is a broken white line separating the lanes
7. **C.** Fog lights
8. **B.** 20 mph
9. **A.** Yield the right-of-way
10. **A.** The first vehicle to arrive
11. **A.** Stop and wait for the train to pass
12. **B.** Arm extended straight out
13. **B.** The right side of the road
14. **A.** Signal your intention and change lanes slowly
15. **A.** 3 feet

Traffic laws and signs exam 5

1. When you see a flashing yellow light at an intersection, you should:

A. ☐ Stop and wait for a green light

B. ☐ Slow down and proceed with caution

C. ☐ Yield the right-of-way to pedestrians and other vehicles

D. ☐ Increase your speed to pass through the intersection quickly

2. When driving in a roundabout, you must:

A. ☐ Stop and wait for a gap in traffic

B. ☐ Yield the right-of-way to vehicles already in the roundabout

C. ☐ Enter the roundabout and proceed with the right-of-way

D. ☐ Signal your intention to exit the roundabout before entering

3. When driving on a highway, you should always:

A. ☐ Drive in the left lane

B. ☐ Drive in the right lane

C. ☐ Drive in the center lane

D. ☐ Drive in the lane with the least traffic

4. When driving on the road with a speed limit of 55 mph, you should drive:

A. ☐ At or below the speed limit

B. ☐ At or above the speed limit

C. ☐ 5 mph over the speed limit

D. ☐ 10 mph over the speed limit

5. When driving on the road with a speed limit of 65 mph, you should drive:

A. ☐ At or below the speed limit

B. ☐ At or above the speed limit

C. ☐ 5 mph over the speed limit

D. ☐ 10 mph over the speed limit

6. What is the minimum distance you must leave between your vehicle and a stopped emergency vehicle with flashing lights?

A. ☐ 100 feet

B. ☐ 200 feet

C. ☐ 300 feet

D. ☐ 400 feet

7. When driving in heavy rain, you should use your:

A. ☐ High beams

B. ☐ Low beams

C. ☐ Fog lights

D. ☐ Hazard lights

8. When driving through a tunnel, you should:

A. ☐ Turn off your headlights.

B. ☐ Use your high beam headlights.

C. ☐ Use your low beam headlights.

D. ☐ Turn on your hazard lights.

9. **When driving on the road with a single lane in each direction and you want to pass a slower-moving vehicle, you should:**

A. ☐ Signal your intention and pass on the right

B. ☐ Signal your intention and pass on the left

C. ☐ Do not signal and pass on the right

D. ☐ Do not signal and pass on the left

10. **When approaching a stop sign, you must:**

A. ☐ Stop and wait for a green light

B. ☐ Slow down and proceed with caution

C. ☐ Come to a complete stop at the designated stop line

D. ☐ Yield the right-of-way to pedestrians and other vehicles

11. **When driving on a two-lane road with a double yellow line, what is the rule for passing other vehicles?**

A. ☐ Always allowed

B. ☐ Only allowed when the vehicle in front is turning left

C. ☐ Never allowed

D. ☐ Only allowed when the vehicle in front is driving below the speed limit

12. **What should you do when you approach a stop sign?**

A. ☐ Come to a complete stop and then proceed when it is safe to do so

B. ☐ Slow down and then proceed through the intersection

C. ☐ Yield to other vehicles and pedestrians and then proceed through the intersection

D. ☐ Continue driving through the intersection without stopping

13. When driving on a highway with multiple lanes, which lane should you be in if you drive at the speed limit?

A. ☐ The left lane

B. ☐ The right lane

C. ☐ The middle lane

D. ☐ Any lane, as long as you are driving at the speed limit

14. What should you do when you see a pedestrian crossing the road at a marked crosswalk?

A. ☐ Ignore the pedestrian and continue driving

B. ☐ Yield to the pedestrian and allow them to cross the road

C. ☐ Honk your horn to warn the pedestrian to get out of the way

D. ☐ Speed up to get through the crosswalk before the pedestrian

15. What is the speed limit in a school zone when children are present?

A. ☐ 15 mph

B. ☐ 25 mph

C. ☐ 35 mph

D. ☐ 45 mph

Correct answers for traffic laws and signs exam 5

1. **B.** Slow down and proceed with caution
2. **B.** Yield the right-of-way to vehicles already in the roundabout
3. **A.** Drive in the left lane
4. **A.** At or below the speed limit
5. **A.** At or below the speed limit
6. **B.** 200 feet
7. **B.** Low beams
8. **C.** Use your low beam headlights.
9. **A.** Signal your intention and pass on the right
10. **C.** Come to a complete stop at the designated stop line
11. **C.** Never allowed
12. **A.** Come to a complete stop and then proceed when it is safe to do so
13. **D.** Any lane, as long as you are driving at the speed limit
14. **B.** Yield to the pedestrian and allow them to cross the road
15. **A.** 15 mph

Vehicle control and safety

Vehicle control and safety is an essential aspects of driving a vehicle. It involves understanding how to safely operate a vehicle, including the proper use of brakes, steering, and acceleration. In this chapter, we will discuss the various techniques and strategies that can help you maintain control of your vehicle and stay safe on the road.

First, let's discuss the importance of maintaining control of your vehicle. When you are driving a car, truck, or any other type of vehicle, it is essential that you have complete control over its movements. This includes stopping, turning, and accelerating safely and efficiently. Losing control of your vehicle can lead to accidents and injuries, so it is essential that you always pay attention to the road and your surroundings and take the necessary precautions to maintain control of your vehicle.

One key aspect of maintaining control of your vehicle is the proper use of brakes. Brakes are an essential safety feature that allows you to stop your vehicle quickly and safely. When you apply the brakes, they work by converting the kinetic energy of your moving vehicle into heat energy. This process slows down the wheels and eventually stops the vehicle. It is essential that you use the brakes correctly, as overbraking or underbraking can both lead to accidents.

Another important aspect of vehicle control is steering. Steering allows you to change the direction of your vehicle and navigate through traffic and around obstacles. It is essential that you have complete control over the steering wheel and can make smooth, precise turns. This can help you avoid accidents and stay safe on the road.

Finally, acceleration is another important aspect of vehicle control. Acceleration is the process of increasing the speed of your vehicle. It is essential that you have complete control over the accelerator pedal and can smoothly and safely accelerate and decelerate as needed. This can help you avoid accidents and maintain a safe speed on the road.

In summary, vehicle control and safety is an essential aspect of driving. It involves understanding how to safely operate a vehicle, including the proper use of brakes, steering, and acceleration. By following the best practices outlined in this chapter, you can maintain control of your vehicle and stay safe on the road.

Welcome to the practice exam on vehicle control and safety! In this exam, you will be tested on your knowledge of how to safely operate a vehicle, including the proper use of brakes, steering, and acceleration. There will be a total of 15 questions, and you will need to answer at least 12 to pass correctly.

We encourage you to thoroughly review and study the relevant materials before attempting the exam. This practice exam is a great opportunity to test your knowledge and identify any areas where you may need further study.

After you have completed the exam, the answers will be provided so that you can check your work and see how you did. Remember, this is a practice exam, so don't worry if you don't get every question right. With dedication and hard work, you can become proficient in vehicle control and safety and be well-prepared for your driving test. Good luck!

For training purposes, you can mark the ☐ symbol next to what you think is the correct answer: Once you have chosen the correct answer, use a pencil or pen to mark the ☐ symbol next to that answer.

Vehicle control and safety exam

1. **What is the correct hand position for gripping the steering wheel while driving?**

    A. ☐ 10 and 2 o'clock

    B. ☐ 8 and 4 o'clock

    C. ☐ 9 and 3 o'clock

    D. ☐ 7 and 5 o'clock

2. **When approaching a stop sign, how far away should you begin to brake?**

    A. ☐ 50 feet

    B. ☐ 100 feet

    C. ☐ 150 feet

    D. ☐ 200 feet

3. **When driving in foggy or rainy conditions, what is the correct way to use your headlights?**

    A. ☐ Use low beams to avoid blinding other drivers

    B. ☐ Use high beams to improve visibility

    C. ☐ Use flashing lights to alert other drivers

    D. ☐ Turn off the headlights to avoid reflection off the water

4. **When driving on a highway, how should you indicate your intention to change lanes?**

    A. ☐ Use your hazard lights

    B. ☐ Use your turn signals

    C. ☐ Honk your horn

    D. ☐ Wave to other drivers

5. **What is the correct way to check for blind spots when changing lanes?**

   A. ☐ Look in the rearview and side mirrors

   B. ☐ Look over your shoulder in the direction you are moving

   C. ☐ Both A and B

   D. ☐ Neither A nor B

6. **When driving in a construction zone, what is the correct speed limit?**

   A. ☐ The posted speed limit

   B. ☐ The speed limit before the construction zone

   C. ☐ The speed limit after the construction zone

   D. ☐ 10 mph below the posted speed limit

7. **What should you do when approaching a pedestrian crossing with a stop sign?**

   A. ☐ Slow down and be prepared to stop

   B. ☐ Continue driving without stopping

   C. ☐ Honk your horn to alert pedestrians

   D. ☐ Drive around the stop sign

8. **What should you do if you are involved in a minor collision?**

   A. ☐ Leave the scene of the accident

   B. ☐ Exchange information with the other driver

   C. ☐ Wait for the police to arrive before exchanging information

   D. ☐ Argue with the other driver

9. **What should you do if you are driving in heavy rain and your visibility is severely limited?**

   A. ☐ Pull over to the side of the road and wait for the rain to pass

   B. ☐ Continue driving at the same speed

   C. ☐ Turn on your hazard lights and drive slowly

   D. ☐ Increase your speed to get through the rain faster

10. **How should you react if a tire blows out while driving?**

   A. ☐ Panic and slam on the brakes

   B. ☐ Steer in the direction the car is pulling

   C. ☐ Slowly and steadily bring the car to a stop

   D. ☐ Accelerate to try to get the car to stop shaking

11. **What should you do if your car starts to fishtail on a wet road?**

   A. ☐ Steer in the direction of the fishtail

   B. ☐ Brake hard and steer in the direction of the fishtail

   C. ☐ Accelerate and steer in the direction of the fishtail

   D. ☐ Brake hard and steer in the opposite direction of the fishtail

12. **What should you do if you are driving and a pedestrian signals that they want to cross the street?**

   A. ☐ Ignore the pedestrian and continue driving

   B. ☐ Stop and let the pedestrian cross

   C. ☐ Speed up to get through the crosswalk before the pedestrian

   D. ☐ Honk your horn to alert the pedestrian

13. **What should you do if you are driving and come to a railroad crossing with a flashing red light and bells ringing?**

    A. ☐ Slow down and proceed with caution

    B. ☐ Stop and wait for the train to pass

    C. ☐ Speed up to get across the tracks before the train

    D. ☐ Drive around the crossing gates

14. **What should you do if you are driving and see a car approaching from the opposite direction with their headlights on high beam?**

    A. ☐ Flash your headlights to signal the other driver to turn their headlights down

    B. ☐ Look away from the headlights to avoid being blinded

    C. ☐ Turn your headlights off to avoid blinding the other driver

    D. ☐ Turn your headlights on high beam to compete with the other driver

15. **What should you do if you are driving and a child runs into the street in front of your car?**

    A. ☐ Swerve to avoid the child

    B. ☐ Brake hard to stop as quickly as possible

    C. ☐ Accelerate to try to get past the child

    D. ☐ Honk your horn to alert the child

Correct answers for vehicle control and safety exam

1. **A.** 10 and 2 o'clock.

2. **B.** 100 feet away.

3. **A.** low beams to avoid blinding other drivers.

4. **B.** Use your turn signals

5. **C.** Both A and B

6. **D.** 10 mph below the posted speed limit

7. **A.** Slow down and be prepared to stop

8. **B.** Exchange information with the other driver

9. **A.** Pull over to the side of the road and wait for the rain to pass

10.   **C.** Slowly and steadily bring the car to a stop

11.   **D.** Brake hard and steer in the opposite direction of the fishtail.

12.   **B.** Stop and let the pedestrian cross

13.   **B.** Stop and wait for the train to pass

14.   **A.** Flash your headlights to signal the other driver to turn their headlights down

15.   **B.** Brake hard to stop as quickly as possible

Vehicle control and safety exam 2

1. **What should you do when driving on a highway and approaching an exit ramp?**

   A. ☐ Stay in the left lane

   B. ☐ Slow down and move to the right lane

   C. ☐ Speed up and pass other cars

   D. ☐ Stay in the center lane

2. **What should you do if you are driving and your brakes fail?**

   A. ☐ Panic and slam on the brakes

   B. ☐ Shift into a lower gear to slow down

   C. ☐ Turn the steering wheel sharply to try to stop the car

   D. ☐ Use the emergency brake to bring the car to a stop

3. **When driving in the rain, what should you do to increase visibility?**

   A. ☐ Turn off your headlights

   B. ☐ Use high beams

   C. ☐ Use windshield wipers and defroster

   D. ☐ Use low beams

4. **When driving on a two-lane road, how far should you be from the car in front of you?**

   A. ☐ One car length

   B. ☐ Two car lengths

   C. ☐ Three car lengths

   D. ☐ Four car lengths

5. **What should you do when approaching a pedestrian in a crosswalk?**

A. ☐ Honk your horn to warn them

B. ☐ Speed up to get through the crosswalk quickly

C. ☐ Stop and let them cross

D. ☐ Swerve around them

6. **When driving on a two-lane road, how much space should you leave when passing a vehicle?**

A. ☐ As little as possible

B. ☐ At least one car length for every 10 mph you are traveling

C. ☐ At least one car length for every 15 mph you are traveling

D. ☐ At least one car length for every 20 mph you are traveling

7. **How can you reduce your risk of hydroplaning on a wet road?**

A. ☐ Increase your speed

B. ☐ Reduce your speed and increase your following distance

C. ☐ Use your brakes frequently

D. ☐ Drive in the left lane

8. **When driving in fog, what should you use to improve your visibility?**

A. ☐ High beams

B. ☐ Low beams

C. ☐ Fog lights

D. ☐ Flashing headlights

9. **When driving at night, what should you do to reduce glare?**

A. ☐ Use high beams

B. ☐ Use low beams

C. ☐ Wear polarized sunglasses

D. ☐ Look away from oncoming headlights

10. **What should you do if you start to skid on a slippery road surface?**

A. ☐ Ease off the accelerator and steer in the direction of the skid

B. ☐ Brake hard and steer in the direction of the skid

C. ☐ Accelerate and steer in the direction of the skid

D. ☐ Brake hard and steer in the opposite direction of the skid

11. **When driving in a heavy rainstorm, what should you do to improve visibility?**

A. ☐ Use high beams

B. ☐ Use low beams

C. ☐ Turn on your hazard lights

D. ☐ Turn off your headlights

12. **When driving on a slippery road, how should you brake?**

A. ☐ Brake as hard as possible

B. ☐ Brake gently to avoid skidding

C. ☐ Use the emergency brake

D. ☐ Alternate between the brake and the accelerator

13. **When driving on a steep downhill, what should you do to maintain control of your vehicle?**

A. ☐ Use the brakes frequently to slow down

B. ☐ Shift into a lower gear to help control your speed

C. ☐ Keep your foot on the accelerator to maintain speed

D. ☐ Shift into a higher gear to go faster

14. **When driving in a school zone, what should you do when you see a school bus with its red lights flashing?**

A. ☐ Pass the bus as quickly as possible

B. ☐ Slow down and be prepared to stop

C. ☐ Honk your horn to alert the bus driver

D. ☐ Swerve around the bus

15. **What should you do if you start to lose traction while driving on a snow-covered road?**

A. ☐ Steer in the direction of the skid

B. ☐ Brake hard and steer in the direction of the skid

C. ☐ Accelerate and steer in the direction of the skid

D. ☐ Ease off the accelerator and steer in the opposite direction of the skid

Correct answers for vehicle control and safety exam 2

1. **B.** Slow down and move to the right lane.

2. **D.** Use the emergency brake to bring the car to a stop

3. **C.** Use windshield wipers and defroster.

4. **C.** Three car lengths

5. **C.** Stop and let them cross.

6. **D.** At least one car length for every 20 mph you are traveling

7. **B.** Reduce your speed and increase your following distance.

8. **C.** Fog lights.

9. **D.** Look away from oncoming headlights.

10. **A.** Ease off the accelerator and steer in the direction of the skid.

11. **B.** Use low beams.

12. **B.** Brake gently to avoid skidding.

13. **B.** Shift into a lower gear to help control your speed.

14. **B.** Slow down and be prepared to stop.

15. **D.** Ease off the accelerator and steer in the opposite direction of the skid.

Vehicle control and safety exam 3

1.   **When driving in a roundabout, what should you do when you see a yield sign?**

   A. ☐ Slow down and be prepared to stop

   B. ☐ Speed up and pass other cars

   C. ☐ Merge into the roundabout without stopping

   D. ☐ Stop and wait for a gap in traffic

2.   **When driving on a highway, what should you do if you need to change lanes?**

   A. ☐ Use your turn signal and merge into the lane

   B. ☐ Honk your horn and merge into the lane

   C. ☐ Cut off other drivers to merge into the lane

   D. ☐ Merge into the lane without signaling

3.   **When driving in a construction zone, what should you do if you see a flagger signaling you to stop?**

   A. ☐ Ignore the flagger and continue driving

   B. ☐ Stop and wait for further instructions

   C. ☐ Honk your horn to show your frustration

   D. ☐ Speed up to get through the construction zone quickly

4.   **What should you do if you are driving and your car starts to skid on ice or snow?**

   A. ☐ Turn the steering wheel in the direction of the skid

   B. ☐ Brake hard to stop the car

   C. ☐ Shift into a lower gear

   D. ☐ Ease off the accelerator and steer in the direction you want the front of the car to go

5.   **When driving in a residential area, what should you do when you see a pedestrian crossing the street at a marked crosswalk?**

    A. ☐ Ignore the pedestrian and continue driving

    B. ☐ Speed up to get through the crosswalk quickly

    C. ☐ Stop and let the pedestrian cross

    D. ☐ Swerve around the pedestrian

6.   **When driving on a slippery road, what should you do to avoid skidding?**

    A. ☐ Brake hard and steer in the direction of the skid

    B. ☐ Accelerate and steer in the direction of the skid

    C. ☐ Ease off the accelerator and steer in the direction of the skid

    D. ☐ Brake hard and steer in the opposite direction of the skid

7.   **How can you reduce your risk of a rollover accident?**

    A. ☐ Avoid sharp turns and sudden movements

    B. ☐ Increase your speed

    C. ☐ Decrease your speed

    D. ☐ Carry a heavy load in the trunk

8.   **When driving on a wet road, what should you do to avoid hydroplaning?**

    A. ☐ Increase your speed

    B. ☐ Reduce your speed and increase your following distance

    C. ☐ Use your brakes frequently

    D. ☐ Drive in the left lane

9. **When driving on a highway, what should you do if you see a car with its hazard lights on?**

   A. ☐ Ignore the car and continue driving

   B. ☐ Speed up and pass the car

   C. ☐ Slow down and be prepared to stop

   D. ☐ Swerve around the car

10. **When driving on a mountain road, what should you do when you approach a turn?**

    A. ☐ Brake before the turn

    B. ☐ Accelerate through the turn

    C. ☐ Downshift before the turn

    D. ☐ Maintain a steady speed through the turn

11. **When driving in a construction zone, what should you do if you see a sign that says "Men Working"?**

    A. ☐ Ignore the sign and continue driving

    B. ☐ Slow down and be prepared to stop

    C. ☐ Speed up and get through the construction zone quickly

    D. ☐ Swerve around the construction workers

12. **What should you do if you start to lose control of your car on a slippery road?**

    A. ☐ Panic and try to regain control by steering sharply

    B. ☐ Accelerate to try and regain control

    C. ☐ Ease off the accelerator and steer in the direction of the skid

    D. ☐ Brake hard and steer in the direction of the skid

13. **What should you do if you are driving and your car starts to skid on a slippery surface?**

    A. ☐ Steer in the direction you want the car to go

    B. ☐ Steer in the opposite direction of the skid

    C. ☐ Brake hard to try to stop the skid

    D. ☐ Accelerate to try to get out of the skid

14. **What is the first step to take when approaching an intersection while driving?**

    A. ☐ Slow down and come to a complete stop

    B. ☐ Check for oncoming traffic and pedestrians

    C. ☐ Turn on your hazard lights

    D. ☐ Honk your horn

15. **When driving on a highway and approaching an exit ramp, what should you do?**

    A. ☐ Stay in the left lane

    B. ☐ Slow down and move to the right lane

    C. ☐ Speed up and pass other cars

    D. ☐ Stay in the center lane

Correct answers for vehicle control and safety exam 3

1. **D.** Stop and wait for a gap in traffic.
2. **A.** Use your turn signal and merge into the lane.
3. **B.** Stop and wait for further instructions.
4. **D.** Ease off the accelerator and steer in the direction you want the front of the car to go
5. **C.** Stop and let the pedestrian cross.
6. **C.** Ease off the accelerator and steer in the direction of the skid.
7. **A.** Avoid sharp turns and sudden movements.
8. **B.** Reduce your speed and increase your following distance.
9. **C.** Slow down and be prepared to stop.
10. **D.** Maintain a steady speed through the turn.
11. **B.** Slow down and be prepared to stop.
12. **C.** Ease off the accelerator and steer in the direction of the skid.
13. **A.** Steer in the direction you want the car to go
14. **B.** Check for oncoming traffic and pedestrians
15. **B.** Slow down and move to the right lane.

Vehicle control and safety exam 4

1. **When driving in wet or slippery conditions, what should you do to maintain control of your vehicle?**

    A. ☐ Increase your speed

    B. ☐ Apply the brakes suddenly

    C. ☐ Avoid sudden movements and reduce your speed

    D. ☐ Ignore the wet or slippery conditions and drive as you normally would

2. **What should you do if you are driving on a highway and your car begins to hydroplane?**

    A. ☐ Accelerate to regain traction

    B. ☐ Brake hard to stop the car

    C. ☐ Steer in the direction of the skid

    D. ☐ Gently ease off the accelerator and steer straight ahead

3. **When driving in fog, what should you do to improve visibility?**

    A. ☐ Turn on your high beam headlights

    B. ☐ Use your fog lights only

    C. ☐ Follow the taillights of the car ahead of you

    D. ☐ Turn on your hazard lights

4. **What should you do if you experience a tire blowout while driving?**

    A. ☐ Brake suddenly and try to steer to the side of the road

    B. ☐ Maintain control of the vehicle and slowly come to a stop

    C. ☐ Accelerate to try and get to your destination as quickly as possible

    D. ☐ Ignore the tire blowout and continue driving

5. What should you do if you are involved in a minor collision while driving?

A. ☐ Leave the scene as quickly as possible

B. ☐ Exchange information with the other driver and report the collision to the authorities if necessary

C. ☐ Agree to handle the damages privately without involving the authorities

D. ☐ Ignore the collision and continue driving

6. What should you do if your car starts to overheat while driving?

A. ☐ Continue driving and hope the problem resolves itself

B. ☐ Pull over to the side of the road and turn off the engine

C. ☐ Open the hood to allow the heat to escape

D. ☐ Turn on the heater to try and cool down the engine

7. What should you do if you are driving and you encounter a pedestrian in a crosswalk?

A. ☐ Honk your horn to get the pedestrian to move out of the way

B. ☐ Accelerate to pass the pedestrian quickly

C. ☐ Slow down and yield to the pedestrian

D. ☐ Swerve around the pedestrian

8. What should you do if you are driving and you see a school bus with its red lights flashing and stop arm extended?

A. ☐ Slow down and proceed with caution

B. ☐ Stop and wait for the stop arm to retract

C. ☐ Pass the bus at a safe distance

D. ☐ Stop and wait until all passengers have exited the bus

9. When driving on a highway, what should you do if you see a car in your rearview mirror signaling to pass you?

A. ☐ Speed up to prevent the car from passing

B. ☐ Flash your headlights to signal that it is okay to pass

C. ☐ Move to the right lane to allow the car to pass

D. ☐ Honk your horn to signal your disapproval

10. What should you do if your vehicle's engine stalls while driving?

A. ☐ Apply the brakes and come to a stop

B. ☐ Shift into a lower gear to slow down

C. ☐ Turn off the ignition and coast to a stop

D. ☐ Use the emergency brake to stop the vehicle

11. What should you do if you are driving and a traffic light turns yellow as you approach an intersection?

A. ☐ Stop immediately

B. ☐ Accelerate to beat the red light

C. ☐ Continue through the intersection at your current speed

D. ☐ Slow down and proceed with caution

12. When driving in snow or ice, what should you do to maintain control of your vehicle?

A. ☐ Increase your speed to get through the snow or ice as quickly as possible

B. ☐ Apply the brakes suddenly to slow down

C. ☐ Avoid sudden movements and reduce your speed

D. ☐ Ignore the snow or ice and drive as you normally would

13. What should you do if your vehicle starts to slide on a slippery road?

A. ☐ Steer in the direction you want the vehicle to go

B. ☐ Steer in the opposite direction of the slide

C. ☐ Apply the brakes

D. ☐ Accelerate to try and regain control

14. When driving in a residential area, what is the proper speed limit?

A. ☐ 15 mph

B. ☐ 25 mph

C. ☐ 35 mph

D. ☐ 45 mph

15. What should you do if you are driving and a tire blows out?

A. ☐ Steer in the direction of the blowout

B. ☐ Brake hard to stop the car

C. ☐ Hold the steering wheel firmly and ease off the accelerator

D. ☐ Shift into a lower gear

Correct answers for vehicle control and safety exam 4

1. **C.** Avoid sudden movements and reduce your speed

2. **D.** Gently ease off the accelerator and steer straight ahead

3. **B.** Use your fog lights only

4. **B.** Maintain control of the vehicle and slowly come to a stop

5. **B.** Exchange information with the other driver and report the collision to the authorities if necessary

6. **B.** Pull over to the side of the road and turn off the engine

7. **C.** Slow down and yield to the pedestrian

8. **D.** Stop and wait until all passengers have exited the bus

9. **C.** Move to the right lane to allow the car to pass

10. **A.** Apply the brakes and come to a stop

11. **C.** Continue through the intersection at your current speed

12. **C.** Avoid sudden movements and reduce your speed

13. **A.** Steer in the direction you want the vehicle to go

14. **B.** 25 mph

15. **C.** Hold the steering wheel firmly and ease off the accelerator

Vehicle control and safety exam 5

1. **When driving in heavy rain, what should you do to increase visibility?**

   A. ☐ Turn on your high beams

   B. ☐ Turn on your hazard lights

   C. ☐ Use your wipers and turn on your headlights

   D. ☐ Slow down and keep a greater following distance from the vehicle in front of you

2. **When driving on a highway, what should you do if you see a car with a flashing hazard light on the side of the road?**

   A. ☐ Slow down and move over to the next lane if possible

   B. ☐ Speed up to get around the stopped vehicle

   C. ☐ Ignore the flashing hazard light and continue driving

   D. ☐ Pull over to the side of the road and stop

3. **If you are driving on a highway and your vehicle starts to hydroplane, what should you do?**

   A. ☐ Apply the brakes suddenly to slow down

   B. ☐ Steer in the direction you want the vehicle to go

   C. ☐ Steer in the opposite direction of the hydroplane

   D. ☐ Maintain control of the vehicle and slowly reduce your speed

4. **When driving in foggy conditions, what should you do to increase visibility?**

   A. ☐ Turn on your high beams

   B. ☐ Turn on your hazard lights

   C. ☐ Use your wipers and turn on your headlights

   D. ☐ Slow down and keep a greater following distance from the vehicle in front of you

5. **When driving on a highway, what is the proper lane to be in if you are planning to turn left at the next intersection?**

A. ☐ The far left lane

B. ☐ The middle lane

C. ☐ The far right lane

D. ☐ It does not matter, as long as you use your turn signal.

6. **When driving in poor weather conditions, which of the following is the most important safety tip to follow?**

A. ☐ Turn on your hazard lights

B. ☐ Increase your following distance

C. ☐ Use your high beam headlights

D. ☐ Pass other vehicles as quickly as possible

7. **When approaching a school bus that is stopped with its red lights flashing and stop arm extended, which of the following actions should you take?**

A. ☐ Proceed with caution and be prepared to stop

B. ☐ Proceed without slowing down or stopping

C. ☐ Stop and wait until the bus begins moving again

D. ☐ Pass the bus on the right side, if it is safe to do so

8. **If your car starts to skid while driving, which of the following should you do?**

A. ☐ Turn the steering wheel in the direction of the skid

B. ☐ Apply the brakes and try to steer in the opposite direction of the skid

C. ☐ Take your foot off the gas pedal and let the car come to a stop on its own

D. ☐ Shift into a lower gear and continue driving as normal

9. **What should you do if your vehicle's steering fails while driving?**

A. ☐ Turn the steering wheel in the opposite direction of the failure

B. ☐ Apply the brakes and come to a stop

C. ☐ Shift into a lower gear to slow down

D. ☐ Turn off the ignition and coast to a stop

10. **What should you do if your vehicle's accelerator becomes stuck while driving?**

A. ☐ Apply the brakes and come to a stop

B. ☐ Shift into a lower gear to slow down

C. ☐ Turn off the ignition and coast to a stop

D. ☐ Use the emergency brake to stop the vehicle

11. **When driving at night, what is the proper following distance to maintain behind the car in front of you?**

A. ☐ One car length for every 10 mph of speed

B. ☐ Two car lengths for every 10 mph of speed

C. ☐ Three car lengths for every 10 mph of speed

D. ☐ Four car lengths for every 10 mph of speed

12. **When driving on a winding road, what should you do to maintain control of your vehicle?**

A. ☐ Increase your speed to get through the curves more quickly

B. ☐ Apply the brakes suddenly to slow down

C. ☐ Avoid sudden movements and reduce your speed

D. ☐ Ignore the curves and drive as you normally would

13. What should you do if your vehicle starts to skid while driving?

A. ☐ Steer in the direction you want the vehicle to go

B. ☐ Steer in the opposite direction of the skid

C. ☐ Apply the brakes

D. ☐ Accelerate to try and regain control

14. If you are driving on a slippery road and your vehicle starts to slide, what should you do?

A. ☐ Steer in the direction you want the vehicle to go

B. ☐ Steer in the opposite direction of the slide

C. ☐ Apply the brakes

D. ☐ Accelerate to try and regain control

15. What should you do if your vehicle's brakes fail while driving?

A. ☐ Apply the emergency brake

B. ☐ Shift into a lower gear to slow down

C. ☐ Turn off the ignition and coast to a stop

D. ☐ Try to steer to the side of the road and come to a stop

Correct answers for vehicle control and safety exam 5

1. **D.** Slow down and keep a greater following distance from the vehicle in front of you

2. **A.** Slow down and move over to the next lane if possible

3. **D.** Maintain control of the vehicle and slowly reduce your speed

4. **C.** Use your wipers and turn on your headlights

5. **A.** The far left lane

6. **B.** Increase your following distance

7. **A.** Proceed with caution and be prepared to stop

8. **B.** Apply the brakes and try to steer in the opposite direction of the skid

9. **B.** Apply the brakes and come to a stop

10. **A.** Apply the brakes and come to a stop

11. **B.** Two car lengths for every 10 mph of speed

12. **C.** Avoid sudden movements and reduce your speed

13. **A.** Steer in the direction you want the vehicle to go

14. **A.** Steer in the direction you want the vehicle to go

15. **A.** Apply the emergency brake

Alcohol and drugs

Driving under the influence of alcohol and drugs is a serious issue that poses a threat to the safety of individuals on the road. In California, it is illegal to operate a motor vehicle with a blood alcohol concentration (BAC) of 0.08% or higher. The state also has strict laws prohibiting the use of drugs while driving, including prescription and over-the-counter medications that can impair driving ability.

To ensure that individuals are aware of the dangers of driving while impaired and to promote safe driving practices, California requires all new drivers to pass a practice driving test before they can obtain a driver's license. This practice test covers a range of topics, including the effects of alcohol and drugs on driving ability and the state's laws regarding impaired driving.

In this chapter, we will provide a comprehensive overview of alcohol and drug-related laws and regulations in California and the impact they have on driving ability. We will also discuss the consequences of violating these laws and the steps individuals can take to avoid being involved in a crash while under the influence.

The effects of alcohol on driving ability:

Alcohol is a central nervous system depressant that impairs cognitive and physical functions, including coordination, reaction time, and judgment. As a person's BAC increases, their ability to safely operate a motor vehicle decreases.

At low levels of intoxication (BAC of 0.02%-0.049%), a person may experience a slight loss of judgment and an increased tendency to take risks. As the BAC increases, the effects of alcohol become more pronounced, leading to impaired coordination, slowed reaction time, and difficulty focusing on multiple tasks. At high levels of intoxication (BAC of 0.2% or higher), a person may have difficulty standing and may lose consciousness.

It is important to note that alcohol affects individuals differently, and the same level of intoxication can have different effects on different people. Factors such as body weight, gender, and the amount of alcohol consumed can all influence the level of impairment experienced by an individual.

Drugs, including prescription and over-the-counter medications, can also impair driving ability. Some drugs can cause drowsiness, dizziness, or hallucinations, which can make it difficult for a person to safely operate a motor vehicle. It is important to carefully read the labels of any medications you are taking and to follow the instructions for use, including any warnings about operating heavy machinery or driving.

California's impaired driving laws:

In California, it is illegal to operate a motor vehicle with a BAC of 0.08% or higher. This applies to all drivers, including those who hold a commercial driver's license. The state also has a "zero tolerance" policy for drivers under the age of 21, meaning that it is illegal for these individuals to operate a motor vehicle with any detectable amount of alcohol in their system.

In addition to laws related to alcohol, California has strict laws prohibiting the use of drugs while driving. It is illegal to operate a motor vehicle while under the influence of any drug that impairs driving ability. This includes prescription medications, over-the-counter medications, and illegal drugs.

Consequences of violating California's impaired driving laws:

The consequences of violating California's impaired driving laws can be severe. A first-time offense can result in fines, the suspension of a driver's license, and the requirement to attend a drug or alcohol education program. Repeat offenders may face even harsher penalties, including jail time and the installation of an ignition interlock device, which requires the driver to blow into a breathalyzer before the car will start.

To prevent crashes and ensure the safety of all individuals on the road, it is important to avoid driving while under the influence of alcohol or drugs. If you plan on consuming alcohol or taking medications that may impair your driving ability, make arrangements for a designated driver or alternative transportation.

If you find yourself in a situation where you have been drinking and need to drive, it is important to understand that it takes time for the body to metabolize alcohol. The only way to completely sober up is to allow time for the body to process the alcohol. There are no shortcuts, and products such as coffee or cold showers will not sober you up. The best course of action is to wait until you are no longer impaired before getting behind the wheel.

It is also important to remember that the effects of alcohol and drugs can last long after the feeling of intoxication has passed. If you have consumed alcohol or taken medication that may impair your driving ability, it is best to wait until you are no longer under the influence before getting behind the wheel.

For training purposes, you can mark the ☐ symbol next to what you think is the correct answer: Once you have chosen the correct answer, use a pencil or pen to mark the ☐ symbol next to that answer.

Alcohol and drugs exam

1. **Which of the following substances can impair your ability to drive safely?**

    A. ☐ Caffeine

    B. ☐ Prescription medication

    C. ☐ Over-the-counter allergy medication

    D. ☐ All of the above

2. **If you are taking a prescription medication that may affect your ability to drive, what should you do?**

    A. ☐ Drive as usual

    B. ☐ Drive only during the daytime

    C. ☐ Avoid driving altogether

    D. ☐ Drive only short distances

3. **What is the term for a person who has consumed alcohol and is unable to safely operate a vehicle due to impaired judgment and reaction time?**

    A. ☐ Intoxicated

    B. ☐ Impaired

    C. ☐ Inebriated

    D. ☐ Drunk

4. **Which of the following is a common sign of drug impairment?**

    A. ☐ Slurred speech

    B. ☐ Dilated pupils

    C. ☐ Sweating

    D. ☐ All of the above

5.   **What is the term for a person who has consumed a combination of alcohol and drugs?**

A. ☐ Polydrug user

B. ☐ Multidrug user

C. ☐ Polysubstance user

D. ☐ Multisubstance user

6.   **True or false: It is safe to drive after using marijuana because it does not impair driving ability.**

A. ☐ True

B. ☐ False

7.   **Which of the following substances is not a stimulant?**

A. ☐ Cocaine

B. ☐ Methamphetamine

C. ☐ Ecstasy

D. ☐ Heroin

8.   **True or false: It is legal to drive under the influence of prescription drugs as long as they were obtained legally and taken as directed by a doctor.**

A. ☐ True

B. ☐ False

9.   **It is legal to drive with a blood alcohol concentration (BAC) of:**

A. ☐ 0.00%

B. ☐ 0.01%

C. ☐ 0.08%

D. ☐ 0.10%

10. **Which of the following is a common symptom of alcohol intoxication?**

   A. ☐ Slurred speech

   B. ☐ Dry mouth

   C. ☐ Drowsiness

   D. ☐ Increased energy

11. **True or false: It is safe to drink and drive as long as you do not feel intoxicated.**

   A. ☐ True

   B. ☐ False

12. **How long does it typically take for the effects of alcohol to wear off?**

   A. ☐ 30 minutes to an hour

   B. ☐ 1-2 hours

   C. ☐ 2-4 hours

   D. ☐ 4-6 hours

13. **Which of the following is a sign of drug impairment?**

   A. ☐ Bloodshot eyes

   B. ☐ Dilated pupils

   C. ☐ Slurred speech

   D. ☐ All of the above

14. **Which of the following substances is a depressant?**

   A. ☐ Cocaine

   B. ☐ Marijuana

   C. ☐ Ecstasy

   D. ☐ Alcohol

15. **True or False: It is safe to drive after using marijuana.**

   A. ☐ True

   B. ☐ False

Correct answers for alcohol and drugs exam

1. **D.** All of the above
2. **C.** Avoid driving altogether
3. **A.** Intoxicated
4. **D.** All of the above
5. **C.** Polysubstance user
6. **B.** False
7. **D.** Heroin
8. **B.** False
9. **A.** 0.00%
10. **A.** Slurred speech is a common symptom of alcohol intoxication.
11. **B.** False
12. **C.** It typically takes 2-4 hours for the effects of alcohol to wear off.
13. **D.** All of the above (bloodshot eyes, dilated pupils, slurred speech) are signs of drug impairment.
14. **D.** Alcohol is a depressant.
15. **B.** False, It is not safe to drive after using marijuana

Alcohol and drugs exam 2

1.   **What is the term for a person who has developed a physical dependence on a substance, such as alcohol or drugs?**

    A. ☐ Addict

    B. ☐ Abuser

    C. ☐ Dependent

    D. ☐ Substance user

2.   **True or false: It is safe to drive after using over-the-counter cold medicine as long as you do not feel drowsy.**

    A. ☐ True

    B. ☐ False

3.   **Which of the following is a common short-term consequence of drug abuse?**

    A. ☐ Memory loss

    B. ☐ Heart attack

    C. ☐ Psychotic episodes

    D. ☐ All of the above

4.   **True or false: It is safe to drink and drive as long as you are not driving erratically.**
    A. ☐ True

    B. ☐ False

5.   **True or False: It is legal to drive with any amount of alcohol in your system.**

    A. ☐ True

    B. ☐ False

6. True or False: It is safe to drive after taking prescription medication if you feel fine.

    A. ☐ True

    B. ☐ False

7. Which of the following substances can cause hallucinations?

    A. ☐ Alcohol

    B. ☐ Cocaine

    C. ☐ Ecstasy

    D. ☐ PCP

8. Which of the following substances can cause a person to become more alert and awake?

    A. ☐ Alcohol

    B. ☐ Cocaine

    C. ☐ Ecstasy

    D. ☐ Marijuana

9. True or False: It is safe to mix alcohol and prescription medication.

    A. ☐ True

    B. ☐ False

10. What is the legal blood alcohol concentration (BAC) limit for driving in most states in the United States?

    A. ☐ 0.01%

    B. ☐ 0.08%

    C. ☐ 0.10%

    D. ☐ 0.20%

11. **What is the legal blood alcohol concentration (BAC) limit for drivers under the age of 21 in most states in the United States?**

    A. ☐ 0.08%
    B. ☐ 0.10%
    C. ☐ 0.02%
    D. ☐ 0.05%

12. **Which of the following substances is classified as a Schedule I controlled substance in the United States, meaning it has a high potential for abuse and no accepted medical use?**

    A. ☐ Cocaine
    B. ☐ Oxycodone
    C. ☐ Marijuana
    D. ☐ Methamphetamine

13. **True or false: It is safe to drive after using over-the-counter allergy medicine as long as you do not feel drowsy.**

    A. ☐ True
    B. ☐ False

14. **Which of the following is a common sign of alcohol impairment in someone who has consumed a large amount of alcohol in a short period of time?**

    A. ☐ Slurred speech
    B. ☐ Poor balance
    C. ☐ Vomiting
    D. ☐ All of the above

15. **True or false: It is safe to drive under the influence of prescription drugs as long as they are not illegal.**

    A. ☐ True
    B. ☐ False

Correct answers for alcohol and drugs exam 2

1. **C.** Dependent
2. **B.** False
3. **D.** All of the above
4. **B.** False
5. **B.** False, It is not legal to drive with any amount of alcohol in your system.
6. **B.** False, It is not safe to drive after taking prescription medication, even if you feel fine.
7. **B.** It is not safe to drive after taking prescription medication, even if you feel fine.
8. **B.** Cocaine can cause a person to become more alert and awake.
9. **B.** It is not safe to mix alcohol and prescription medication.
10. **B.** 0.08%. In most states in the United States, the legal BAC limit for driving is 0.08%.
11. **C.** 0.02%
12. **C.** Marijuana
13. **B.** False
14. **D.** All of the above
15. **B.** False

Alcohol and drugs exam 3

1. **What is the legal blood alcohol concentration (BAC) limit for drivers in most states in the United States?**

   A. ☐ 0.08%

   B. ☐ 0.10%

   C. ☐ 0.12%

   D. ☐ 0.15%

2. **Which of the following substances is not a depressant?**

   A. ☐ Alcohol

   B. ☐ Marijuana

   C. ☐ Benzodiazepines

   D. ☐ Cocaine

3. **How long does it typically take for alcohol to be completely eliminated from the body?**

   A. ☐ One hour

   B. ☐ Two hours

   C. ☐ Three hours

   D. ☐ It varies depending on the person

4. **If you are under the influence of alcohol, what is the best way to sober up before driving?**

   A. ☐ Drinking coffee

   B. ☐ Taking a cold shower

   C. ☐ Sleeping it off

   D. ☐ None of the above

5.   **Which of the following is a symptom of drug impairment?**

   A. ☐ Slurred speech

   B. ☐ Dizziness

   C. ☐ Poor balance and coordination

   D. ☐ All of the above

6.   **If you are pulled over by a police officer and they suspect that you are impaired by drugs, they may ask you to perform which of the following tests?**

   A. ☐ A breathalyzer test

   B. ☐ A field sobriety test

   C. ☐ A blood test

   D. ☐ All of the above

7.   **If you are arrested for driving under the influence of drugs or alcohol, you may face which of the following consequences?**

   A. ☐ Fines

   B. ☐ Jail time

   C. ☐ Loss of your driver's license

   D. ☐ All of the above

8.   **If you are convicted of a DUI, which of the following may be required as part of your sentence?**

   A. ☐ Alcohol education classes

   B. ☐ Community service

   C. ☐ Installment of an ignition interlock device

   D. ☐ All of the above

9.   **Which of the following is a common sign of alcohol impairment?**

   A. ☐ Poor balance

   B. ☐ Slowed reaction time

   C. ☐ Dilated pupils

   D. ☐ All of the above

10.   **True or false: It is safe to mix alcohol and over-the-counter medications.**

   A. ☐ True

   B. ☐ False

11.   **True or false: It is safe to drink and drive as long as you do not feel drunk.**

   A. ☐ True

   B. ☐ False

12.   **Which of the following is a common long-term consequence of alcohol abuse?**

   A. ☐ Liver damage

   B. ☐ Heart disease

   C. ☐ Brain damage

   D. ☐ All of the above

13.   **True or false: Alcohol is the only substance that can impair driving ability.**

   A. ☐ True

   B. ☐ False

14. **Which of the following substances is a hallucinogen?**

   A. ☐ LSD

   B. ☐ Cocaine

   C. ☐ Methamphetamine

   D. ☐ Marijuana

15. **True or false: It is safe to drive under the influence of prescription drugs as long as they are not listed as impairing on the label.**

   A. ☐ True

   B. ☐ False

Correct answers for alcohol and drugs exam 3

1. **A.** 0.08%
2. **D.** Cocaine
3. **D.** It varies depending on the person
4. **D.** None of the above
5. **D.** All of the above
6. **D.** All of the above
7. **D.** All of the above
8. **D.** All of the above
9. **D.** All of the above
10. **B.** False
11. **B.** False
12. **D.** All of the above
13. **B.** False
14. **A.** LSD
15. **B.** False

Alcohol and drugs exam 4

1. **What is the most common cause of impaired driving?**

   A. ☐ Alcohol
   B. ☐ Prescription medication
   C. ☐ Illegal drugs
   D. ☐ Lack of sleep

2. **How can you reduce the risk of being involved in an impaired driving crash?**

   A. ☐ Drive at a safe speed and maintain a safe following distance
   B. ☐ Wear your seatbelt and make sure all passengers do as well
   C. ☐ Avoid driving when you are tired or have been drinking
   D. ☐ All of the above

3. **What are the effects of alcohol on the body? Select all that apply.**

   A. ☐ Slowed reaction time
   B. ☐ Decreased coordination
   C. ☐ Impaired judgment
   D. ☐ Increased aggression
   E. ☐ All of the above

4. **How long does it typically take for the body to metabolize one standard drink (12 ounces of beer, 5 ounces of wine, or 1.5 ounces of hard liquor)?**

   A. ☐ 15 minutes
   B. ☐ 30 minutes
   C. ☐ 1 hour
   D. ☐ 2 hours

5. **Which of the following drugs can impair your ability to drive safely? Select all that apply.**

A. ☐ Marijuana

B. ☐ Cocaine

C. ☐ Heroin

D. ☐ Methamphetamine

E. ☐ All of the above

6. **Can over-the-counter or prescription medications affect your ability to drive safely?**

A. ☐ No

B. ☐ Yes, but only if taken in large doses

C. ☐ Yes, even if taken as directed

D. ☐ Yes, but only if taken with alcohol

7. **What should you do if you are pulled over by a police officer who suspects you have been driving while impaired?**

A. ☐ Refuse to take a chemical test

B. ☐ Be cooperative and follow the officer's instructions

C. ☐ Try to talk your way out of it

D. ☐ None of the above

8. **Can you be charged with impaired driving if you are under the influence of legal drugs, such as prescription medication or over-the-counter medication?**

A. ☐ No

B. ☐ Yes, but only if the medication was not prescribed to you

C. ☐ Yes, but only if you are also under the influence of alcohol

D. ☐ Yes, regardless of the circumstances.

9. **What is the legal blood alcohol concentration limit for driving in most states in the United States?**

   A. ☐ 0.08%

   B. ☐ 0.10%

   C. ☐ 0.12%

   D. ☐ 0.15%

10. **How long does it typically take for alcohol to be absorbed into the bloodstream?**

    A. ☐ 30 minutes

    B. ☐ 1 hour

    C. ☐ 2 hours

    D. ☐ It varies based on individual factors

11. **Which of the following substances is illegal to consume and operate a motor vehicle under the influence of in all 50 states?**

    A. ☐ Alcohol

    B. ☐ Marijuana

    C. ☐ Prescription medication

    D. ☐ None of the above

12. **Which of the following substances can be detected through a roadside saliva test?**

    A. ☐ Alcohol

    B. ☐ Marijuana

    C. ☐ Cocaine

    D. ☐ All of the above

13. Which of the following substances can be detected through a blood test?

A. ☐ Alcohol

B. ☐ Marijuana

C. ☐ Cocaine

D. ☐ All of the above

14. At what blood alcohol concentration (BAC) are you considered legally intoxicated in most states?

A. ☐ 0.08%

B. ☐ 0.05%

C. ☐ 0.02%

D. ☐ 0.01%

15. What is the best way to sober up after drinking alcohol?

A. ☐ Drink coffee

B. ☐ Take a cold shower

C. ☐ Sleep it off

D. ☐ There is no way to speed up the sobering process

Correct answers for alcohol and drugs exam 4

1. **A.** Alcohol. Alcohol is the most common cause of impaired driving.

2. **D.** All of the above. You can reduce the risk of being involved in an impaired driving crash by driving at a safe speed and maintaining a safe following distance, wearing your seatbelt and making sure all passengers do as well, and avoiding driving when you are tired or have been drinking.

3. **E.** All of the above.

4. **C.** 1 hour. It typically takes the body about 1 hour to metabolize one standard drink.

5. **E.** All of the above. Marijuana, cocaine, heroin, and methamphetamine can all impair your ability to drive safely.

6. **C.** Yes, even if taken as directed.

7. **B.** Be cooperative and follow the officer's instructions.

8. **D.** Yes, regardless of the circumstances.

9. **A.** The legal blood alcohol concentration limit for driving in most states in the United States is 0.08%.

10. **D.** It varies based on individual factors

11. **A.** Alcohol

12. **D.** All of the above

13. **D.** All of the above

14. **A.** 0.08%

15. **D.** There is no way to speed up the sobering process

Alcohol and drugs exam 5

1. **Which of the following substances is a depressant that can impair driving ability?**

A. ☐ Marijuana

B. ☐ Alcohol

C. ☐ Cocaine

D. ☐ Ecstasy

2. **Which of the following substances is illegal to consume and operate a motor vehicle under the influence of?**

A. ☐ Prescription medication

B. ☐ Alcohol

C. ☐ Caffeine

D. ☐ None of the above

3. **Which of the following substances is commonly found in over-the-counter cold and flu medications and can cause drowsiness and impair driving ability?**

A. ☐ Acetaminophen

B. ☐ Dextromethorphan

C. ☐ Pseudoephedrine

D. ☐ All of the above

4. **Which of the following is NOT a symptom of being under the influence of alcohol?**

A. ☐ Slurred speech

B. ☐ Impaired judgment

C. ☐ Faster reflexes

D. ☐ Lack of coordination

5. **Which of the following is NOT a symptom of being under the influence of marijuana?**

   A. ☐ Impaired judgment

   B. ☐ Decreased reaction time

   C. ☐ Increased appetite

   D. ☐ Faster reflexes

6. **Which of the following is NOT a symptom of being under the influence of stimulants such as cocaine or amphetamines?**

   A. ☐ Agitation

   B. ☐ Increased heart rate

   C. ☐ Increased alertness

   D. ☐ Drowsiness

7. **Which of the following is NOT a symptom of being under the influence of prescription opioids such as oxycodone or hydrocodone?**

   A. ☐ Drowsiness

   B. ☐ Confusion

   C. ☐ Nausea

   D. ☐ Increased energy

8. **It is safe to drive under the influence of alcohol as long as you are below the legal blood alcohol concentration limit.**

   A. ☐ True

   B. ☐ False

9. **It is safe to drive under the influence of marijuana as long as you are below the legal limit for THC in your system.**

   A. ☐ True

   B. ☐ False

10. **It is always safe to drive under the influence of prescription medication as long as it is prescribed by a doctor.**

A. ☐ True

B. ☐ False

11. **Which of the following substances can cause hallucinations and impair driving ability?**

A. ☐ Alcohol

B. ☐ Marijuana

C. ☐ LSD

D. ☐ Ecstasy

12. **Which of the following substances can cause drowsiness and impair driving ability?**

A. ☐ Alcohol

B. ☐ Caffeine

C. ☐ Cocaine

D. ☐ Prescription sleeping pills

13. **It is legal to operate a motor vehicle under the influence of prescription medication as long as it is prescribed by a doctor.**

A. ☐ True

B. ☐ False

14. **It is illegal to operate a motor vehicle with a blood alcohol concentration (BAC) of 0.08% or higher in all 50 states.**

A. ☐ True

B. ☐ False

15. It is illegal to operate a motor vehicle with a THC concentration of 5 ng/mL or higher in all 50 states.

A. ☐ True

B. ☐ False

Correct answers for alcohol and drugs exam 5

1. **B.** Alcohol
2. **B.** Alcohol
3. **D.** All of the above
4. **C.** Faster reflexes
5. **D.** Faster reflexes
6. **D.** Drowsiness
7. **D.** Increased energy
8. **B.** False
9. **B.** False
10. **B.** False
11. **C.** LSD
12. **A.** Alcohol
13. **B.** False
14. **A.** True
15. **A.** True

Vehicle equipment and maintenance

Welcome to the chapter on vehicle equipment and maintenance! As a California driver, it is important to have a basic understanding of the various parts of your vehicle and how to properly maintain them. This knowledge not only helps you to keep your vehicle running smoothly and efficiently, but it also helps to ensure your safety on the road.

One key aspect of vehicle equipment and maintenance is knowing the various parts of your vehicle and their functions. This includes understanding the different systems and components that make up your vehicle, such as the engine, transmission, suspension, brakes, and more. By knowing the basic workings of these systems, you can better identify potential issues and take the necessary steps to fix them.

Proper maintenance is also crucial for the smooth operation and longevity of your vehicle. This includes performing regular oil and filter changes, checking and replacing worn out or damaged parts, and keeping your vehicle clean and in good repair. By performing these maintenance tasks, you can help to prevent breakdowns and costly repairs down the road.

In addition to maintaining the various systems and components of your vehicle, it is also important to understand how to safely load and unload your vehicle. This includes properly securing any cargo or passenger belongings and making sure that the weight is evenly distributed in the vehicle. Failing to properly load and unload your vehicle can not only cause damage to the vehicle, but it can also affect its handling and stability on the road, potentially leading to accidents.

Overall, having a basic understanding of vehicle equipment and maintenance is essential for all California drivers. By staying informed and taking the necessary steps to maintain and care for your vehicle, you can help to ensure your safety on the road and prolong the life of your vehicle.

For training purposes, you can mark the ◯ symbol next to what you think is the correct answer: Once you have chosen the correct answer, use a pencil or pen to mark the ◯ symbol next to that answer.

Vehicle equipment and maintenance exam

1.　**What should you do if you notice that your car's tires are balding or have uneven wear?**

　　A. ☐ Ignore it and continue driving as normal

　　B. ☐ Replace the tires immediately

　　C. ☐ Rotate the tires to distribute the wear evenly

　　D. ☐ Check the tire pressure and adjust as needed

2.　**How often should you check the fluid levels in your vehicle?**

　　A. ☐ Every week

　　B. ☐ Every month

　　C. ☐ Every three months

　　D. ☐ Every six months

3.　**What should you do if you notice that your car's brakes are making a squealing noise?**

　　A. ☐ Ignore it and continue driving as normal

　　B. ☐ Check the brake fluid level and refill if necessary

　　C. ☐ Have the brakes checked and potentially replaced by a mechanic

　　D. ☐ Adjust the brake pads to eliminate the noise

4.　**Which of the following is NOT a step in the pre-trip inspection of a vehicle?**

　　A. ☐ Checking tire pressure

　　B. ☐ Checking the fuel level

　　C. ☐ Checking the transmission fluid level

　　D. ☐ Checking the engine oil level

5. **What should you do if you notice that your car's engine is overheating?**

A. ☐ Ignore it and continue driving as normal

B. ☐ Turn off the air conditioning to reduce the load on the engine

C. ☐ Pull over and turn off the engine to let it cool down

D. ☐ Check the coolant level and refill if necessary

6. **What should you do if you notice that your car's battery is dead?**

A. ☐ Check the battery terminals for corrosion and clean them if necessary

B. ☐ Replace the battery with a new one

C. ☐ Jump start the battery and drive around to recharge it

D. ☐ Charge the battery with a battery charger

7. **What should you do if you notice that your car's wipers are not working properly?**

A. ☐ Ignore it and continue driving as normal

B. ☐ Replace the wipers with new ones

C. ☐ Clean the wipers and the windshield

D. ☐ Adjust the wipers to a different setting

8. **Which of the following is NOT a potential consequence of neglecting to properly maintain a vehicle?**

A. ☐ Decreased fuel efficiency

B. ☐ Increased risk of mechanical failure

C. ☐ Improved vehicle performance

D. ☐ Decreased emissions

9. **What should you do if you notice that your car's headlights are not working properly?**

    A. ☐ Ignore it and continue driving as normal

    B. ☐ Check the fuse and replace it if necessary

    C. ☐ Replace the headlights with new ones

    D. ☐ Adjust the headlights to a different setting

10. **How often should you rotate the tires on your vehicle?**

    A. ☐ Every 1,000 miles

    B. ☐ Every 3,000 miles

    C. ☐ Every 5,000 miles

    D. ☐ Every 7,500 miles

11. **What should you do if you notice that your car's fuel economy has decreased significantly?**

    A. ☐ Ignore it and continue driving as normal

    B. ☐ Check the air filter and replace it if necessary

    C. ☐ Check the spark plugs and replace them if necessary

    D. ☐ All of the above

12. **Which of the following is NOT a recommended practice when changing a tire?**

    A. ☐ Using a lug wrench to loosen the lug nuts before lifting the vehicle

    B. ☐ Placing the spare tire on the ground in front of the flat tire

    C. ☐ Lifting the vehicle using a hydraulic jack

    D. ☐ Tightening the lug nuts in a star pattern to ensure even pressure on the tire

13. **What should you do if you notice that your car's transmission is slipping?**

   A. ☐ Ignore it and continue driving as normal
   B. ☐ Check the transmission fluid level and refill if necessary
   C. ☐ Have the transmission checked and potentially repaired or replaced by a mechanic
   D. ☐ Adjust the transmission to a different setting

14. **How often should you change the transmission fluid in your vehicle?**

   A. ☐ Every 1,000 miles
   B. ☐ Every 3,000 miles
   C. ☐ Every 5,000 miles
   D. ☐ Every 7,500 miles

15. **What should you do if you notice that your car's power steering is not working properly?**

   A. ☐ Ignore it and continue driving as normal
   B. ☐ Check the power steering fluid level and refill if necessary
   C. ☐ Have the power steering checked and potentially repaired or replaced by a mechanic
   D. ☐ Adjust the power steering to a different setting

Correct answers for vehicle equipment and maintenance exam

1. **B.** Replace the tires immediately

2. **B**. Every month

3. **C.** Have the brakes checked and potentially replaced by a mechanic

4. **C.** Checking the transmission fluid level is not a step in the pre-trip inspection of a vehicle.

5. **C.** Pull over and turn off the engine to let it cool down

6. **B.** Replace the battery with a new one

7. **B.** Replace the wipers with new ones

8. **A.** Decreased fuel efficiency is a potential consequence of neglecting to properly maintain a vehicle.

9. **C.** Replace the headlights with new ones

10. **C.** Every 5,000 miles

11. **D.** All of the above

12. **A.** Using a lug wrench to loosen the lug nuts before lifting the vehicle is a recommended practice when changing a tire.

13. **C.** Have the transmission checked and potentially repaired or replaced by a mechanic

14. **D.** Every 7,500 miles

15. **C.** Have the power steering checked and potentially repaired or replaced by a mechanic

Vehicle equipment and maintenance exam 2

1. **How often should you check the alignment of your vehicle's wheels?**

    A. ☐ Every 1,000 miles

    B. ☐ Every 3,000 miles

    C. ☐ Every 5,000 miles

    D. ☐ Every 7,500 miles

2. **What should you do if you notice that your car's suspension is not working properly?**

    A. ☐ Ignore it and continue driving as normal

    B. ☐ Check the suspension fluid level and refill if necessary

    C. ☐ Have the suspension checked and potentially repaired or replaced by a mechanic

    D. ☐ Adjust the suspension to a different setting

3. **How often should you check the brake fluid in your vehicle?**

    A. ☐ Every 1,000 miles

    B. ☐ Every 3,000 miles

    C. ☐ Every 5,000 miles

    D. ☐ Every 7,500 miles

4. **What should you do if you notice that your car's exhaust is making an unusual noise?**

    A. ☐ Ignore it and continue driving as normal

    B. ☐ Check the exhaust pipe and muffler for damage and repair or replace as necessary

    C. ☐ Have the exhaust system checked and potentially repaired or replaced by a mechanic

    D. ☐ Adjust the exhaust to a different setting

5.   **How often should you check the air conditioning system in your vehicle?**

    A. ☐ Every 1,000 miles

    B. ☐ Every 3,000 miles

    C. ☐ Every 5,000 miles

    D. ☐ Every 7,500 miles

6.   **What should you do if you notice that your car's steering wheel is shaking or vibrating while driving?**

    A. ☐ Ignore it and continue driving as normal

    B. ☐ Check the tire pressure and adjust as needed

    C. ☐ Have the wheels balanced or the tires rotated

    D. ☐ All of the above

7.   **How often should you check the engine oil level in your vehicle?**

    A. ☐ Every week

    B. ☐ Every month

    C. ☐ Every three months

    D. ☐ Every six months

8.   **What should you do if you notice that your car's engine is making a knocking or tapping noise?**

    A. ☐ Ignore it and continue driving as normal

    B. ☐ Check the engine oil level and refill if necessary

    C. ☐ Have the engine checked and potentially repaired or replaced by a mechanic

    D. ☐ Adjust the engine to a different setting

9. **How often should you check the condition of your vehicle's belts and hoses?**

   A. ☐ Every 1,000 miles

   B. ☐ Every 3,000 miles

   C. ☐ Every 5,000 miles

   D. ☐ Every 7,500 miles

10. **What should you do if you notice that your car's steering is stiff or unresponsive?**

    A. ☐ Ignore it and continue driving as normal

    B. ☐ Check the steering fluid level and refill if necessary

    C. ☐ Have the steering system checked and potentially repaired or replaced by a mechanic

    D. ☐ Adjust the steering to a different setting

11. **How often should you check the condition of your vehicle's spark plugs?**

    A. ☐ Every 1,000 miles

    B. ☐ Every 3,000 miles

    C. ☐ Every 5,000 miles

    D. ☐ Every 7,500 miles

12. **What should you do if you notice that your car's suspension is making a knocking or clunking noise while driving?**

    A. ☐ Ignore it and continue driving as normal

    B. ☐ Check the suspension fluid level and refill if necessary

    C. ☐ Have the suspension system checked and potentially repaired or replaced by a mechanic

    D. ☐ Adjust the suspension to a different setting

13. **How often should you check the condition of your vehicle's air conditioning system?**

    A. ☐ Every 1,000 miles

    B. ☐ Every 3,000 miles

    C. ☐ Every 5,000 miles

    D. ☐ Every 7,500 miles

14. **What should you do if you notice that your car's transmission is making a grinding or whining noise while driving?**

    A. ☐ Ignore it and continue driving as normal

    B. ☐ Check the transmission fluid level and refill if necessary

    C. ☐ Have the transmission system checked and potentially repaired or replaced by a mechanic

    D. ☐ Adjust the transmission to a different setting

15. **How often should you check the condition of your vehicle's fuel system?**

    A. ☐ Every 1,000 miles

    B. ☐ Every 3,000 miles

    C. ☐ Every 5,000 miles

    D. ☐ Every 7,500 miles

Correct answers for Vehicle equipment and maintenance exam 2

1. **C.** Every 5,000 miles
2. **C.** Have the suspension checked and potentially repaired or replaced by a mechanic
3. **C.** Every 5,000 miles
4. **C.** Have the exhaust system checked and potentially repaired or replaced by a mechanic
5. **C.** Every 5,000 miles
6. **D.** All of the above
7. **B.** Every month
8. **C.** Have the engine checked and potentially repaired or replaced by a mechanic
9. **C.** Every 5,000 miles
10. **C.** Have the steering system checked and potentially repaired or replaced by a mechanic
11. **C.** Every 5,000 miles
12. **C.** Have the suspension system checked and potentially repaired or replaced by a mechanic
13. **C.** Every 5,000 miles
14. **C.** Have the transmission system checked and potentially repaired or replaced by a mechanic
15. **C.** Every 5,000 miles

Vehicle equipment and maintenance exam 3

1.   **What should you do if you notice that your car's dashboard warning lights are illuminated?**

   A. ☐ Ignore them and continue driving as normal

   B. ☐ Check the owner's manual for information on the warning lights

   C. ☐ Have the vehicle checked and potentially repaired by a mechanic

   D. ☐ All of the above

2.   **How often should you check the condition of your vehicle's battery?**

   A. ☐ Every week

   B. ☐ Every month

   C. ☐ Every three months

   D. ☐ Every six months

3.   **What should you do if you notice that your car's engine is running rough or misfiring?**

   A. ☐ Ignore it and continue driving as normal

   B. ☐ Check the spark plugs and replace them if necessary

   C. ☐ Have the engine checked and potentially repaired or replaced by a mechanic

   D. ☐ Adjust the engine to a different setting

4.   **How often should you check the condition of your vehicle's brakes?**

   A. ☐ Every 1,000 miles

   B. ☐ Every 3,000 miles

   C. ☐ Every 5,000 miles

   D. ☐ Every 7,500 miles

5.   **What should you do if you notice that your car's wheels are out of alignment?**

A. ☐ Ignore it and continue driving as normal

B. ☐ Have the wheels aligned by a mechanic

C. ☐ Adjust the alignment yourself

D. ☐ Check the owner's manual for instructions on how to adjust the alignment

6.   **How often should you check the condition of your vehicle's tires?**

A. ☐ Every 1,000 miles

B. ☐ Every 3,000 miles

C. ☐ Every 5,000 miles

D. ☐ Every 7,500 miles

7.   **What should you do if you notice that your car's transmission is not shifting smoothly?**

A. ☐ Ignore it and continue driving as normal

B. ☐ Check the transmission fluid level and refill if necessary

C. ☐ Have the transmission system checked and potentially repaired or replaced by a mechanic

D. ☐ Adjust the transmission to a different setting

8.   **How often should you check the condition of your vehicle's steering system?**

A. ☐ Every 1,000 miles

B. ☐ Every 3,000 miles

C. ☐ Every 5,000 miles

D. ☐ Every 7,500 miles

9.   **What should you do if you notice that your car's suspension is not providing a smooth ride?**

    A. ☐ Ignore it and continue driving as normal

    B. ☐ Check the suspension fluid level and refill if necessary

    C. ☐ Have the suspension system checked and potentially repaired or replaced by a mechanic

    D. ☐ Adjust the suspension to a different setting

10.   **How often should you check the condition of your vehicle's exhaust system?**

    A. ☐ Every 1,000 miles

    B. ☐ Every 3,000 miles

    C. ☐ Every 5,000 miles

    D. ☐ Every 7,500 miles

11.   **What should you do if you notice that your car's doors or windows are not functioning properly?**

    A. ☐ Ignore it and continue driving as normal

    B. ☐ Check the door or window mechanism for damage and repair or replace as necessary

    C. ☐ Have the door or window system checked and potentially repaired or replaced by a mechanic

    D. ☐ Adjust the door or window to a different setting

12.   **How often should you check the condition of your vehicle's electrical system?**

    A. ☐ Every week

    B. ☐ Every month

    C. ☐ Every three months

    D. ☐ Every six months

13. **What should you do if you notice that your car's air conditioning is not functioning properly?**

    A. ☐ Ignore it and continue driving as normal

    B. ☐ Check the air conditioning system for damage and repair or replace as necessary

    C. ☐ Have the air conditioning system checked and potentially repaired or replaced by a mechanic

    D. ☐ Adjust the air conditioning to a different setting

14. **How often should you check the condition of your vehicle's body and paint?**

    A. ☐ Every 1,000 miles

    B. ☐ Every 3,000 miles

    C. ☐ Every 5,000 miles

    D. ☐ Every 7,500 miles

15. **What should you do if you notice that your car's engine is consuming an abnormal amount of oil?**

    A. ☐ Ignore it and continue driving as normal

    B. ☐ Check the engine oil level and refill as necessary

    C. ☐ Have the engine checked and potentially repaired or replaced by a mechanic

    D. ☐ Adjust the engine to a different setting

Correct answers for vehicle equipment and maintenance exam 3

1. **D.** All of the above
2. **B.** Every month
3. **C.** Have the engine checked and potentially repaired or replaced by a mechanic
4. **C.** Every 5,000 miles
5. **B.** Have the wheels aligned by a mechanic
6. **C.** Every 5,000 miles
7. **C.** Have the transmission system checked and potentially repaired or replaced by a mechanic
8. **C.** Every 5,000 miles
9. **C.** Have the suspension system checked and potentially repaired or replaced by a mechanic
10. **C.** Every 5,000 miles
11. **C.** Have the door or window system checked and potentially repaired or replaced by a mechanic
12. **B.** Every month
13. **C.** Have the air conditioning system checked and potentially repaired or replaced by a mechanic
14. **C.** Every 5,000 miles
15. **C.** Have the engine checked and potentially repaired or replaced by a mechanic

Vehicle equipment and maintenance exam 4

1. **What should be checked during a routine vehicle maintenance check?**

A. ☐ Oil levels

B. ☐ Tire pressure

C. ☐ Transmission fluid levels

D. ☐ All of the above

2. **How often should you rotate your tires?**

A. ☐ Every 5,000 miles

B. ☐ Every 10,000 miles

C. ☐ Every 15,000 miles

D. ☐ Every 20,000 miles

3. **What is the purpose of a muffler on a vehicle?**

A. ☐ To reduce engine noise

B. ☐ To increase horsepower

C. ☐ To improve fuel efficiency

D. ☐ To improve handling

4. **How often should you change the oil in your vehicle?**

A. ☐ Every 3,000 miles

B. ☐ Every 5,000 miles

C. ☐ Every 7,500 miles

D. ☐ Every 10,000 miles

5. What is the purpose of a timing belt in a vehicle?

A. ☐ To transfer power from the engine to the transmission

B. ☐ To synchronize the movement of the valves and pistons

C. ☐ To keep the wheels aligned

D. ☐ To keep the vehicle stable while driving

6. What should you do if your vehicle's check engine light comes on?

A. ☐ Ignore it and continue driving

B. ☐ Check the oil levels and tire pressure

C. ☐ Take the vehicle to a mechanic as soon as possible

D. ☐ Check the gas cap to make sure it is tightened properly

7. How often should you check the brake fluid level in your vehicle?

A. ☐ Every month

B. ☐ Every 3 months

C. ☐ Every 6 months

D. ☐ Every year

8. What is the purpose of a catalytic converter in a vehicle?

A. ☐ To reduce emissions

B. ☐ To improve fuel efficiency

C. ☐ To increase horsepower

D. ☐ To improve handling

9. **What should you do if your vehicle's brakes feel spongy or unresponsive?**

A. ☐ Ignore it and continue driving

B. ☐ Check the brake fluid level

C. ☐ Take the vehicle to a mechanic as soon as possible

D. ☐ Check the alignment of the wheels

10. **How often should you check the air filter in your vehicle?**

A. ☐ Every month

B. ☐ Every 3 months

C. ☐ Every 6 months

D. ☐ Every year

11. **What is the purpose of an oxygen sensor in a vehicle?**

A. ☐ To monitor and control the air-fuel ratio in the engine

B. ☐ To reduce emissions

C. ☐ To improve fuel efficiency

D. ☐ To increase horsepower

12. **How often should you check the coolant level in your vehicle?**

A. ☐ Every month

B. ☐ Every 3 months

C. ☐ Every 6 months

D. ☐ Every year

13. What is the purpose of a drive belt in a vehicle?

A. ☐ To transfer power from the engine to the transmission

B. ☐ To synchronize the movement of the valves and pistons

C. ☐ To power the alternator, water pump, and other accessories

D. ☐ To keep the vehicle stable while driving

14. What should you do if your vehicle's tires are bald or have uneven wear?

A. ☐ Ignore it and continue driving

B. ☐ Check the tire pressure

C. ☐ Take the vehicle to a mechanic as soon as possible

D. ☐ Replace the tires

15. How often should you check the power steering fluid level in your vehicle?

A. ☐ Every month

B. ☐ Every 3 months

C. ☐ Every 6 months

D. ☐ Every year

Correct answers for vehicle equipment and maintenance exam 4

1. D. All of the above (oil levels, tire pressure, and transmission fluid levels should all be checked during a routine vehicle maintenance check)

2. B. Every 10,000 miles (it is generally recommended to rotate your tires every 10,000 miles to ensure even wear)

3. A. To reduce engine noise (the muffler is a part of the exhaust system that helps to reduce the noise produced by the engine)

4. B. Every 5,000 miles (it is generally recommended to change the oil in your vehicle every 5,000 miles, or at least once a year)

5. B. To synchronize the movement of the valves and pistons (the timing belt is a critical part of the engine that helps to synchronize the movement of the valves and pistons)

6. C. Take the vehicle to a mechanic as soon as possible (if the check engine light comes on, it is important to have the vehicle checked by a mechanic as soon as possible to diagnose and fix any potential issues)

7. A. Every month (it is important to check the brake fluid level in your vehicle regularly to ensure that it is at the correct level and to catch any potential issues before they become serious problems)

8. A. To reduce emissions (the catalytic converter is a part of the exhaust system that helps to reduce the emissions produced by the vehicle)

9. C. Take the vehicle to a mechanic as soon as possible (if the brakes feel spongy or unresponsive, it is important to have the vehicle checked by a mechanic as soon as possible to diagnose and fix any potential issues)

10. C. Every 6 months (it is generally recommended to check the air filter in your vehicle every 6 months or every time you change the oil)

11. A. To monitor and control the air-fuel ratio in the engine (the oxygen sensor is a part of the emissions system that helps to monitor and control the air-fuel ratio in the engine)

12. A. Every month (it is important to check the coolant level in your vehicle regularly to ensure that it is at the correct level and to catch any potential issues before they become serious problems)

13. C. To power the alternator, water pump, and other accessories (the drive belt is a critical part of the engine that helps to power the alternator, water pump, and other accessories)

14. D. Replace the tires (if the tires are bald or have uneven wear, it is important to replace them to ensure the safety and proper operation of the vehicle)

15. B. Every 3 months (it is generally recommended to check the power steering fluid level in your vehicle every 3 months or every time you change the oil)

Vehicle equipment and maintenance exam 5

1. **What is the purpose of spark plugs in a vehicle?**

A. ☐ To ignite the fuel in the engine

B. ☐ To reduce emissions

C. ☐ To improve fuel efficiency

D. ☐ To increase horsepower

2. **How often should you check the battery in your vehicle?**

A. ☐ Every month

B. ☐ Every 3 months

C. ☐ Every 6 months

D. ☐ Every year

3. **What should you do if your vehicle's steering is hard to turn or feels loose?**

A. ☐ Ignore it and continue driving

B. ☐ Check the power steering fluid level

C. ☐ Take the vehicle to a mechanic as soon as possible

D. ☐ Check the alignment of the wheels

4. **How often should you check the transmission fluid level in your vehicle?**

A. ☐ Every month

B. ☐ Every 3 months

C. ☐ Every 6 months

D. ☐ Every year

5. **What is the purpose of a fuel filter in a vehicle?**

A. ☐ To remove contaminants from the fuel

B. ☐ To reduce emissions

C. ☐ To improve fuel efficiency

D. ☐ To increase horsepower

6. **How often should you check the belts and hoses in your vehicle?**

A. ☐ Every month

B. ☐ Every 3 months

C. ☐ Every 6 months

D. ☐ Every year

7. **What should you do if your vehicle's tires are underinflated or overinflated?**

A. ☐ Ignore it and continue driving

B. ☐ Check the tire pressure

C. ☐ Take the vehicle to a mechanic as soon as possible

D. ☐ Replace the tires

8. **How often should you check the wiper blades in your vehicle?**

A. ☐ Every month

B. ☐ Every 3 months

C. ☐ Every 6 months

D. ☐ Every year

9. What should you do if your vehicle's engine is overheating?

A. ☐ Ignore it and continue driving

B. ☐ Check the coolant level

C. ☐ Take the vehicle to a mechanic as soon as possible

D. ☐ Check the alignment of the wheels

10. How often should you check the oil level in your vehicle?

A. ☐ Every month

B. ☐ Every 3 months

C. ☐ Every 6 months

D. ☐ Every year

11. What is the purpose of a fuel pump in a vehicle?

A. ☐ To transfer fuel from the tank to the engine

B. ☐ To reduce emissions

C. ☐ To improve fuel efficiency

D. ☐ To increase horsepower

12. How often should you check the brakes in your vehicle?

A. ☐ Every month

B. ☐ Every 3 months

C. ☐ Every 6 months

D. ☐ Every year

13. What should you do if your vehicle's tires are out of balance?

A. ☐ Ignore it and continue driving

B. ☐ Check the tire pressure

C. ☐ Take the vehicle to a mechanic as soon as possible

D. ☐ Rotate the tires

14. What is the purpose of a timing chain in a vehicle?

A. ☐ To transfer power from the engine to the transmission

B. ☐ To synchronize the movement of the valves and pistons

C. ☐ To keep the wheels aligned

D. ☐ To keep the vehicle stable while driving

15. How often should you check the suspension in your vehicle?

A. ☐ Every month

B. ☐ Every 3 months

C. ☐ Every 6 months

D. ☐ Every year

Correct answers for vehicle equipment and maintenance exam 5

1. **A.** To ignite the fuel in the engine (spark plugs are a critical part of the ignition system that helps to ignite the fuel in the engine)

2. **A.** Every month (it is important to check the battery in your vehicle regularly to ensure that it is in good condition and to catch any potential issues before they become serious problems)

3. **C.** Take the vehicle to a mechanic as soon as possible (if the steering is hard to turn or feels loose, it is important to have the vehicle checked by a mechanic as soon as possible to diagnose and fix any potential issues)

4. **A.** Every month (it is important to check the transmission fluid level in your vehicle regularly to ensure that it is at the correct level and to catch any potential issues before they become serious problems)

5. **A.** To remove contaminants from the fuel (the fuel filter is a part of the fuel system that helps to remove contaminants from the fuel)

6. **C.** Every 6 months (it is generally recommended to check the belts and hoses in your vehicle every 6 months or every time you change the oil)

7. **B.** Check the tire pressure (if the tires are underinflated or overinflated, it is important to adjust the tire pressure to the recommended level to ensure the safety and proper operation of the vehicle)

8. **C.** Every 6 months (it is generally recommended to check the wiper blades in your vehicle every 6 months or whenever they appear to be worn or damaged)

9. **C.** Take the vehicle to a mechanic as soon as possible (if the engine is overheating, it is important to have the vehicle checked by a mechanic as soon as possible to diagnose and fix any potential issues)

10. **A.** Every month (it is important to check the oil level in your vehicle regularly to ensure that it is at the correct level and to catch any potential issues before they become serious problems)

11. **A.** To transfer fuel from the tank to the engine (the fuel pump is a part of the fuel system that helps to transfer fuel from the tank to the engine)

12. **A.** Every month (it is important to check the brakes in your vehicle regularly to ensure that they are in good condition and to catch any potential issues before they become serious problems)

13. D. Rotate the tires (if the tires are out of balance, it is important to rotate them to ensure even wear and to improve the performance and handling of the vehicle)

14. B. To synchronize the movement of the valves and pistons (the timing chain is a critical part of the engine that helps to synchronize the movement of the valves and pistons)

15. B. Every 3 months (it is generally recommended to check the suspension in your vehicle every 3 months or every time you change the oil)

Sharing the road

Sharing the road is an essential aspect of safe driving. In California, it is important for all drivers to understand and follow the rules of the road in order to prevent accidents and ensure the safety of everyone on the road. One way to learn and practice these rules is through the California Practice Driving Tests, which are designed to help drivers prepare for the actual driving test and understand the rules and regulations of the road.

In this chapter, we will provide an overview of the California Practice Driving Tests and how they can help you become a safer and more confident driver. We will discuss the types of tests available, the importance of practicing and preparing for the tests, and the benefits of passing the tests.

Types of California practice driving tests

There are several types of California Practice Driving Tests available to drivers. These tests are designed to help drivers understand and practice the rules of the road, as well as prepare for the actual driving test.

The first type of practice driving test is the written test. This test consists of multiple-choice questions that cover a variety of topics related to driving, such as traffic laws, road signs, and safe driving practices. The written test is typically taken on a computer at the Department of Motor Vehicles (DMV) or online through the DMV's website.

The second type of practice driving test is the behind-the-wheel test. This test is also known as the road test and is typically taken at the DMV or at a licensed driving school. The behind-the-wheel test assesses a driver's ability to safely operate a vehicle on the road, including their ability to follow traffic laws, signals, and signs, as well as their ability to safely maneuver the vehicle.

Importance of practicing and preparing for the California practice driving tests

It is important for drivers to practice and prepare for the California practice driving tests in order to become safe and confident drivers. Taking the time to study and practice for the tests can help drivers understand the rules of the road and make informed decisions when driving.

Additionally, practicing for the tests can help drivers feel more confident and prepared for the actual driving test. This can help reduce anxiety and improve performance on the test.

Benefits of Passing the California Practice Driving Tests

Passing the California Practice Driving Tests has several benefits for drivers. First and foremost, it demonstrates that a driver has a solid understanding of the rules of the road and is capable of safely operating a vehicle. This can help drivers feel more confident and secure on the road and can also help reduce the risk of accidents.

In addition to the personal benefits of passing the tests, there are also practical benefits. For example, passing the tests is often a requirement for obtaining a driver's license or permit. In California, drivers must pass the written test and the behind-the-wheel test in order to obtain a driver's license.

Conclusion

The California Practice Driving Tests are an important tool for helping drivers understand and practice the rules of the road. By taking the time to study and prepare for the tests, drivers can become safer and more confident on the road. Additionally, passing the tests has numerous personal and practical benefits, including the ability to obtain a driver's license.

For training purposes, you can mark the ☐ symbol next to what you think is the correct answer: Once you have chosen the correct answer, use a pencil or pen to mark the ☐ symbol next to that answer.

Sharing the road exam

1. **What should you do if you are approaching an intersection and the traffic light is red?**

   A. ☐ Stop and wait for the light to turn green

   B. ☐ Proceed through the intersection if there are no other cars present

   C. ☐ Make a right turn without stopping unless there are signs prohibiting the turn

   D. ☐ Accelerate through the intersection as quickly as possible

2. **When driving in fog, you should:**

   A. ☐ Use your high beam headlights

   B. ☐ Use your low beam headlights

   C. ☐ Turn off your headlights

   D. ☐ Use your hazard lights

3. **When driving in a roundabout, which of the following is correct?**

   A. ☐ You must yield to all vehicles already in the roundabout.

   B. ☐ You have the right-of-way over all vehicles already in the roundabout.

   C. ☐ You must stop and wait for all vehicles already in the roundabout to exit before entering.

   D. ☐ You can enter the roundabout at any time, regardless of the presence of other vehicles.

4. **When driving on a highway with a posted speed limit of 65 mph, you should:**

   A. ☐ Drive as fast as you feel comfortable.

   B. ☐ Drive at or below the posted speed limit.

   C. ☐ Drive as fast as possible to get to your destination faster.

   D. ☐ Drive at or above the posted speed limit.

5. When driving behind a school bus that is picking up or dropping off children, you must:

A. ☐ Slow down and be prepared to stop.

B. ☐ Pass the school bus as quickly as possible.

C. ☐ Ignore the school bus and continue driving at the same speed.

D. ☐ Use your horn to alert the school bus driver to your presence.

6. When driving on a highway, you should use your turn signal:

A. ☐ Only when changing lanes

B. ☐ Only when turning

C. ☐ Both when changing lanes and when turning

D. ☐ Never, it is not necessary

7. When two vehicles arrive at a four-way stop intersection at the same time, who has the right of way?

A. ☐ The vehicle on the right

B. ☐ The vehicle on the left

C. ☐ The vehicle going straight

D. ☐ The vehicle turning left

8. If you are driving on the road with two lanes in each direction and you want to turn left at the next intersection, which lane should you be in?

A. ☐ The left lane

B. ☐ The right lane

C. ☐ Either lane is acceptable

D. ☐ It depends on the traffic flow

9. When approaching a pedestrian in a crosswalk, you should:

A. ☐ Speed up and get through the crosswalk as quickly as possible

B. ☐ Come to a complete stop and wait for the pedestrian to cross

C. ☐ Honk your horn to signal the pedestrian to get out of the way

D. ☐ Swerve around the pedestrian

10. When driving in inclement weather, you should:

A. ☐ Drive at the same speed as you would in clear conditions.

B. ☐ Increase your following distance.

C. ☐ Use your high beam headlights.

D. ☐ Decrease your following distance.

11. When approaching a pedestrian who is using a white cane or a guide dog, you should:

A. ☐ Stop and wait for the pedestrian to cross the street.

B. ☐ Slow down and be prepared to stop.

C. ☐ Honk your horn to alert the pedestrian to your presence.

D. ☐ Ignore the pedestrian and continue driving at the same speed.

12. When driving on the highway, you should use your turn signal when:

A. ☐ Changing lanes

B. ☐ Turning at an intersection

C. ☐ Both A and B

D. ☐ Neither A nor B

13. When approaching a stopped emergency vehicle with flashing lights, you should:

A. ☐ Continue driving at the same speed.

B. ☐ Slow down and proceed with caution.

C. ☐ Stop and wait for the emergency vehicle to pass.

D. ☐ Increase your speed and pass the emergency vehicle as quickly as possible.

14. When driving in a construction zone, you should:

A. ☐ Stop and yield to all traffic before entering the roundabout

B. ☐ Enter the roundabout and take the first available exit

C. ☐ Enter the roundabout and continue driving until you reach your desired exit

D. ☐ All of the above

15. You are driving on a two-lane road and you see a school bus with its red lights flashing and stop arm extended on the other side of the road. You should:

A. ☐ Slow down and be prepared to stop if necessary

B. ☐ Keep driving, as the school bus is on the other side of the road

C. ☐ Pass the school bus as quickly as possible

D. ☐ Pull over to the side of the road and stop

Correct answers for sharing the road exam

1. **A.** Stop and wait for the light to turn green
2. **B.** Use your low beam headlights
3. **A.** You must yield to all vehicles already in the roundabout.
4. **B.** Drive at or below the posted speed limit.
5. **A.** Slow down and be prepared to stop.
6. **C.** Both when changing lanes and when turning
7. **A.** The vehicle on the right has the right of way
8. **A.** The left lane
9. **B.** Come to a complete stop and wait for the pedestrian to cross
10. **B.** Increase your following distance.
11. **A.** Stop and wait for the pedestrian to cross the street.
12. **C.** Both A and B
13. **C.** Stop and wait for the emergency vehicle to pass.
14. **C.** Enter the roundabout and continue driving until you reach your desired exit
15. **A.** Slow down and be prepared to stop if necessary

Sharing the road exam 2

1. **You are driving on a highway and you see a vehicle with its hazard lights on pulled over to the side of the road. You should:**

   A. ☐ Ignore the vehicle and continue driving

   B. ☐ Slow down and move to the far lane

   C. ☐ Speed up and get past the vehicle as quickly as possible

   D. ☐ Stop and offer assistance if it is safe to do so

2. **When approaching a stopped emergency vehicle with its lights activated, you should:**

   A. ☐ Slow down and proceed with caution

   B. ☐ Stop and wait until the emergency vehicle moves on

   C. ☐ Speed up and get past the emergency vehicle as quickly as possible

   D. ☐ All of the above

3. **When driving on a two-lane road, you should:**

   A. ☐ Stay in the right lane at all times

   B. ☐ Use the left lane to pass slower vehicles

   C. ☐ Use the right lane to pass slower vehicles

   D. ☐ All of the above

4. **When driving on a road with a center turn lane, you should:**

   A. ☐ Use the center turn lane to pass slower vehicles

   B. ☐ Never use the center turn lane for any reason

   C. ☐ Only use the center turn lane to make a left turn

   D. ☐ Use the center turn lane to turn right at the next intersection

5. When driving on a highway, you should use your turn signal when:

A. ☐ Changing lanes

B. ☐ Turning at an intersection

C. ☐ Both A and B

D. ☐ Neither A nor B

6. When driving in a school zone, you should:

A. ☐ Drive the speed limit or faster

B. ☐ Honk your horn to warn pedestrians

C. ☐ Drive slowly and be extra cautious

D. ☐ All of the above

7. When driving on a multi-lane road, you should:

A. ☐ Drive in the left lane at all times

B. ☐ Stay in the right lane unless passing

C. ☐ Always drive in the center lane

D. ☐ None of the above

8. When driving at night, it is important to:

A. ☐ Keep your high beams on at all times

B. ☐ Use your high beams to blind oncoming drivers

C. ☐ Use your low beams to improve visibility

D. ☐ None of the above

9. When approaching a pedestrian crossing, you should:

A. ☐ Slow down and be ready to stop

B. ☐ Speed up to get through the crossing quickly

C. ☐ Honk your horn to warn the pedestrian

D. ☐ All of the above

10. When driving in a roundabout, you should:

A. ☐ Stop and yield to all traffic before entering the roundabout

B. ☐ Enter the roundabout and take the first available exit

C. ☐ Enter the roundabout and continue driving until you reach your desired exit

D. ☐ All of the above

11. When driving on a two-lane road, you should:

A. ☐ Stay in the right lane at all times

B. ☐ Use the left lane to pass slower vehicles

C. ☐ Use the right lane to pass slower vehicles

D. ☐ All of the above

12. When driving in bad weather, it is important to:

A. ☐ Increase your following distance

B. ☐ Use your high beams to improve visibility

C. ☐ Drive faster to get to your destination quicker

D. ☐ All of the above

13. When driving on a road with a posted speed limit of 35 mph, you should:

A. ☐ Always drive at the posted speed limit, regardless of the traffic flow

B. ☐ Drive at a speed that is safe and appropriate for the road conditions

C. ☐ Drive as fast as you can to get to your destination as quickly as possible

D. ☐ Drive at a speed that is 5 mph over the posted speed limit

14. When driving in heavy rain, you should:

A. ☐ Increase your following distance

B. ☐ Decrease your following distance

C. ☐ Keep the same following distance as you would normally

D. ☐ Increase your speed to get through the rain as quickly as possible

15. When driving in heavy rain, it is important to:

A. ☐ Turn off your windshield wipers

B. ☐ Use your hazard lights

C. ☐ Decrease your speed and increase your following distance

D. ☐ None of the above

Correct answers for sharing the road exam 2

1. **B.** Slow down and move to the far lane
2. **B.** Stop and wait until the emergency vehicle moves on
3. **B.** Use the left lane to pass slower vehicles
4. **C.** Only use the center turn lane to make a left turn
5. **C.** Both A and B
6. **C.** Drive slowly and be extra cautious
7. **B.** Stay in the right lane unless passing
8. **C.** Use your low beams to improve visibility
9. **A.** Slow down and be ready to stop
10. **C.** Enter the roundabout and continue driving until you reach your desired exit
11. **B.** Use the left lane to pass slower vehicles
12. **A.** Increase your following distance
13. **B.** Drive at a speed that is safe and appropriate for the road conditions
14. **A.** Increase your following distance
15. **C.** Decrease your speed and increase your following distance

Sharing the road exam 3

1. **When driving on a highway with multiple lanes, you should:**

   A. ☐ Use the left lane for passing only

   B. ☐ Stay in the right lane unless passing

   C. ☐ Use any lane to pass slower vehicles

   D. ☐ None of the above

2. **When approaching a pedestrian at a marked crosswalk, which of the following actions is required by law?**

   A. ☐ Slow down and honk your horn as you pass

   B. ☐ Stop and wait for the pedestrian to cross

   C. ☐ Increase your speed to get through the crosswalk quickly

   D. ☐ Swerve around the pedestrian and continue driving

3. **When driving behind a school bus, you should:**

   A. ☐ Increase your following distance

   B. ☐ Pass the school bus as quickly as possible

   C. ☐ Stay close to the school bus so it doesn't have to stop

   D. ☐ None of the above

4. **When driving on the road with a speed limit of 55 mph, you should:**

   A. ☐ Drive as fast as you can

   B. ☐ Drive the speed limit or slower

   C. ☐ Drive the speed limit or faster

   D. ☐ None of the above

5. **When approaching a stopped school bus with its red lights flashing, you must:**

A. ☐ Stop at least 50 feet behind the bus

B. ☐ Slow down and proceed with caution

C. ☐ Stop at least 10 feet behind the bus

D. ☐ Continue driving, as the bus is not on your side of the road

6. **If you approach an intersection with a traffic signal that is not working, you should:**

A. ☐ Treat it as a four-way stop

B. ☐ Proceed with caution, as you have the right-of-way

C. ☐ Yield to any pedestrians or vehicles already in the intersection

D. ☐ Come to a full stop and then proceed when it is safe

7. **When driving on a highway with multiple lanes going in the same direction, you should:**

A. ☐ Always stay in the left lane

B. ☐ Stay in the right lane unless passing another vehicle

C. ☐ Use any lane that is available

D. ☐ Only use the center lane for turning

8. **If you are driving on a road with two lanes in each direction, and you want to turn left at an upcoming intersection, you should:**

A. ☐ Signal and turn from the right lane

B. ☐ Stop and wait until the emergency vehicle moves on

C. ☐ Speed up and get past the emergency vehicle as quickly as possible

D. ☐ All of the above

9. When driving on a highway, you should:

A. ☐ Always use the left lane for passing

B. ☐ Signal and turn from the left lane

C. ☐ Signal and turn from the center lane

D. ☐ Not signal and turn from whichever lane is most convenient

10. When driving on a highway, it is important to:

A. ☐ Use your turn signal when changing lanes

B. ☐ Stay in the left lane at all times

C. ☐ Use the right lane for passing only

D. ☐ None of the above

11. When driving on a road with a posted speed limit of 55 mph, you should:

A. ☐ Always drive at least 5 mph over the speed limit

B. ☐ Only drive the posted speed limit if traffic is heavy

C. ☐ Drive the speed that is appropriate for the road and weather conditions

D. ☐ Only drive the posted speed limit if you are in a residential area

12. When driving on a winding road, you should:

A. ☐ Speed up to get through the curves faster

B. ☐ Stay in the center of the lane to maintain control of your vehicle

C. ☐ Use your horn to alert other drivers to your presence

D. ☐ Slow down and allow plenty of space between you and other vehicles

13. When driving on a multi-lane road, which lane should you be in if you are driving slower than other traffic?

A. ☐ The left lane

B. ☐ The right lane

C. ☐ Any lane, as long as you are driving the speed limit

D. ☐ The middle lane

14. When driving in a construction zone, which of the following is required?

A. ☐ Slowing down to the posted speed limit

B. ☐ Merging into a single lane when directed by a construction worker

C. ☐ Ignoring detour signs and driving through the construction zone as quickly as possible

D. ☐ Driving in the left lane, even if it is not the fastest lane

15. When you see a pedestrian in a crosswalk, you should:

A. ☐ Stop and let the pedestrian cross

B. ☐ Slow down and proceed with caution

C. ☐ Honk your horn to alert the pedestrian to your presence

D. ☐ Swerve around the pedestrian and continue driving

Correct answers for sharing the road exam 3

1.   **A.** Use the left lane for passing only

2.   **B.** Stop and wait for the pedestrian to cross

3.   **A.** Increase your following distance

4.   **C.** Drive the speed limit or faster

5.   **A.** Stop at least 50 feet behind the bus

6.   **A.** Treat it as a four-way stop

7.   **C.** Use any lane that is available

8.   **B.** Stop and wait until the emergency vehicle moves on

9.   **B.** Signal and turn from the left lane

10. **A.** Use your turn signal when changing lanes

11. **C.** Drive the speed that is appropriate for the road and weather conditions

12. **D.** Slow down and allow plenty of space between you and other vehicles

13. **B.** The right lane

14. **A.** Slowing down to the posted speed limit

15. **A.** Stop and let the pedestrian cross

Sharing the road exam 4

1. **If you are driving on a multi-lane road and want to turn left at the next intersection, you should:**

A. ☐ Signal and turn from the left lane

B. ☐ Signal and turn from the right lane

C. ☐ Signal and turn from the center lane

D. ☐ Not signal, as other drivers should expect you to turn

2. **When driving in heavy traffic, you should:**

A. ☐ Follow other vehicles closely to avoid being cut off

B. ☐ Maintain a safe following distance

C. ☐ Weave in and out of lanes to get ahead

D. ☐ Honk your horn frequently to alert other drivers

3. **When approaching a school bus that is stopped and has its flashing red lights activated, what should you do?**

A. ☐ Pass the school bus on the right side

B. ☐ Slow down and proceed with caution

C. ☐ Stop and wait until the flashing red lights are turned off

D. ☐ Continue driving at the same speed

4. **When driving on a two-lane road and a vehicle ahead of you is turning left, what should you do?**

A. ☐ Speed up and pass on the right

B. ☐ Slow down and prepare to stop

C. ☐ Honk your horn to alert the turning vehicle

D. ☐ Pass on the left after checking for oncoming traffic

5. When driving on a highway, you should use your high beam headlights:

A. ☐ Whenever there is no oncoming traffic

B. ☐ Whenever there are no other vehicles nearby

C. ☐ Whenever the weather is foggy or rainy

D. ☐ Never

6. When approaching a roundabout, you should:

A. ☐ Slow down and yield to pedestrians and vehicles already in the roundabout

B. ☐ Speed up to get through the roundabout quickly

C. ☐ Honk your horn to alert other drivers

D. ☐ All of the above

7. If you are driving on a two-lane road and want to pass another vehicle, you should:

A. ☐ Signal and pass on the left

B. ☐ Signal and pass on the right

C. ☐ Not signal, as other drivers should expect you to pass

D. ☐ Honk your horn before passing

8. If you are driving on a highway and see an emergency vehicle approaching with its lights and sirens activated, you should:

A. ☐ Pull over to the right side of the road and stop

B. ☐ Speed up to get out of the way

C. ☐ Honk your horn to alert the emergency vehicle

D. ☐ All of the above

9. When driving on the road with a speed limit of 55 mph, what should you do if you see a police officer on the side of the road with a radar gun?

A. ☐ Speed up to avoid getting pulled over

B. ☐ Slow down to the posted speed limit

C. ☐ Continue driving at your current speed

D. ☐ Wave to the police officer

10. If you are driving and encounter a school bus that is stopped with its red lights flashing and stop sign extended, you should:

A. ☐ Stop and wait for the red lights to turn off before proceeding

B. ☐ Pass the school bus at a safe distance

C. ☐ Honk your horn to alert the school bus driver

D. ☐ All of the above

11. When driving on a two-way street, what should you do if you see a car approaching from the opposite direction with its headlights on a high beam?

A. ☐ Turn your headlights on high beam

B. ☐ Flash your headlights to signal the other driver to turn their headlights down

C. ☐ Turn your headlights off

D. ☐ Shield your eyes and continue driving

12. When driving on the road with a speed limit of 35 mph, what should you do if you see a pedestrian walking on the side of the road?

A. ☐ Speed up to get past the pedestrian quickly

B. ☐ Slow down and give the pedestrian plenty of room

C. ☐ Honk your horn to alert the pedestrian

D. ☐ Swerve around the pedestrian

13. When driving in adverse weather conditions, you should:

A. ☐ Increase your following distance

B. ☐ Decrease your following distance

C. ☐ Drive as you normally would

D. ☐ Honk your horn frequently to alert other drivers

14. When driving in a roundabout, what should you do if you see a pedestrian crossing the road ahead?

A. ☐ Continue driving and honk your horn

B. ☐ Stop and wait for the pedestrian to cross

C. ☐ Speed up and pass the pedestrian

D. ☐ Swerve around the pedestrian

15. When driving in inclement weather, what should you do if you start to hydroplane?

A. ☐ Brake hard and steer in the direction you want to go

B. ☐ Accelerate and steer in the direction you want to go

C. ☐ Take your foot off the gas and steer in the direction you want to go

D. ☐ Brake hard and steer in the opposite direction you want to go

Correct answers for sharing the road exam 4

1. **B.** Signal and turn from the right lane
2. **B.** Maintain a safe following distance
3. **C.** Stop and wait until the flashing red lights are turned off
4. **D.** Pass on the left after checking for oncoming traffic
5. **D.** Never
6. **A.** The vehicle entering the roundabout
7. **A.** Signal and pass on the left
8. **A.** Pull over to the right side of the road and stop
9. **B.** Slow down to the posted speed limit
10. **A.** Stop and wait for the red lights to turn off before proceeding
11. **B.** Flash your headlights to signal the other driver to turn their headlights down
12. **B.** Slow down and give the pedestrian plenty of room
13. **A.** Increase your following distance
14. **B.** Stop and wait for the pedestrian to cross
15. **C.** Take your foot off the gas and steer in the direction you want to go

Sharing the road exam 5

1. **When driving on a road with a speed limit of 50 mph, what should you do if you see a school bus ahead with its stop sign extended and flashing red lights activated?**

A. ☐ Pass the school bus on the right side

B. ☐ Slow down and proceed with caution

C. ☐ top and wait until the flashing red lights are turned off

D. ☐ Continue driving at the same speed

2. **When driving on a two-way street and a vehicle ahead of you is turning left, what should you do?**

A. ☐ Speed up and pass on the right

B. ☐ Slow down and prepare to stop

C. ☐ Honk your horn to alert the turning vehicle

D. ☐ Pass on the left after checking for oncoming traffic

3. **If you are driving and see a pedestrian using a white cane or guide dog, you should:**

A. ☐ Slow down and be prepared to stop

B. ☐ Speed up to get past the pedestrian quickly

C. ☐ Honk your horn to alert the pedestrian

D. ☐ All of the above

4. **When driving in a residential area, you should always:**

A. ☐ Drive as fast as you can

B. ☐ Follow the posted speed limit

C. ☐ Drive slower than the posted speed limit

D. ☐ Drive faster than the posted speed limit

5. If you are driving and approach a traffic light that has malfunctioned and is not functioning, you should:

A. ☐ Treat the intersection as a four-way stop

B. ☐ Treat the intersection as a yield sign

C. ☐ Treat the intersection as a regular traffic light

D. ☐ Ignore the intersection and continue driving

6. If you are driving on a highway and see a construction zone ahead, you should:

A. ☐ Ignore the reduced speed limit and continue driving at your normal speed

B. ☐ Follow the posted speed limit

C. ☐ Drive slower than the posted speed limit

D. ☐ Drive faster than the posted speed limit

7. When driving on a multi-lane road and you need to change lanes, what should you do?

A. ☐ Use your turn signal and merge into the new lane

B. ☐ Honk your horn and merge into the new lane

C. ☐ Speed up and cut in front of the other vehicles

D. ☐ Wait until there is a large gap in traffic and then merge

8. When driving in inclement weather, what should you do if you start to skid?

A. ☐ Brake hard and steer in the direction you want to go

B. ☐ Accelerate and steer in the direction you want to go

C. ☐ Take your foot off the gas and steer in the direction you want to go

D. ☐ Brake hard and steer in the opposite direction you want to go

9. **When driving in heavy traffic, how much distance should you leave between your vehicle and the one in front of you?**

A. ☐ One car length

B. ☐ Two car lengths

C. ☐ Three car lengths

D. ☐ Four car lengths

10. **When driving on a road with a divided median, what should you do if you see an animal on the road ahead?**

A. ☐ Swerve around the animal

B. ☐ Slow down and proceed with caution

C. ☐ Stop and wait for the animal to move

D. ☐ Honk your horn to scare the animal away

11. **When driving on the road with a speed limit of 45 mph, what should you do if you see a pedestrian crossing the road ahead?**

A. ☐ Speed up to get past the pedestrian quickly

B. ☐ Slow down and give the pedestrian plenty of room

C. ☐ Honk your horn to alert the pedestrian

D. ☐ Swerve around the pedestrian

12. **When driving on a highway, what should you do if you see a car in front of you with its hazard lights on?**

A. ☐ Pass the car as quickly as possible

B. ☐ Slow down and proceed with caution

C. ☐ Change lanes if possible

D. ☐ Speed up and pass the car on the left

13. When approaching an intersection, what should you do if you see a pedestrian on the crosswalk?

A. ☐ Speed up and pass the pedestrian

B. ☐ Stop and let the pedestrian pass

C. ☐ Continue driving and honk your horn

D. ☐ Swerve around the pedestrian

14. When driving behind a bicycle, what is the recommended distance to follow?

A. ☐ 1-2 car lengths

B. ☐ 3-4 car lengths

C. ☐ 5-6 car lengths

D. ☐ 7 car lengths or more

15. When driving in a roundabout, which vehicle has the right of way?

A. ☐ The vehicle entering the roundabout

B. ☐ The vehicle already in the roundabout

C. ☐ The vehicle with the largest number of passengers

D. ☐ The vehicle that is moving the fastest

Correct answers for sharing the road exam 5

1. **C.** Stop and wait until the flashing red lights are turned off
2. **D.** Pass on the left after checking for oncoming traffic
3. **A.** Slow down and be prepared to stop
4. **B.** Follow the posted speed limit
5. **A.** Treat the intersection as a four-way stop
6. **B.** Follow the posted speed limit
7. **A.** Use your turn signal and merge into the new lane
8. **C.** Take your foot off the gas and steer in the direction you want to go
9. **C.** Three car lengths
10. **B.** Slow down and proceed with caution
11. **B.** Slow down and give the pedestrian plenty of room
12. **B.** Slow down and proceed with caution
13. **B.** Stop and let the pedestrian pass
14. **C.** 5-6 car lengths
15. **A.** The vehicle entering the roundabout

Transportation of hazardous materials

Transportation of hazardous materials is a critical aspect of modern society, as these materials are essential for a wide range of industries, including manufacturing, construction, agriculture, and healthcare. However, the handling and transport of hazardous materials also carries significant risks, including the potential for accidents, spills, and exposure to dangerous substances. As a result, it is important that individuals and organizations involved in the transportation of hazardous materials understand the regulations, safety measures, and best practices for handling these materials safely.

In this chapter, we will provide an overview of the transportation of hazardous materials, including the types of materials that are considered hazardous, the regulations and laws that govern the transport of these materials, and the training and certification required for individuals and organizations involved in the handling and transport of hazardous materials. We will also discuss the various modes of transportation commonly used for hazardous materials, including road, rail, air, and water, and the unique considerations and challenges associated with each mode of transport.

Types of hazardous materials

Hazardous materials are any substances that pose a risk to human health, property, or the environment when they are transported. These materials can be solids, liquids, gases, or mixtures, and they are classified based on the type of hazard they pose. Some common categories of hazardous materials include:

Explosives: Materials that are capable of detonation or rapid combustion, such as dynamite, fireworks, and certain types of ammunition.

Flammables: Materials that are easily ignited and burn rapidly, such as gasoline, alcohol, and certain types of paints and solvents.

Oxidizers: Materials that can release oxygen or other oxidizing agents, potentially causing fires or explosions, such as chlorine and other bleach products.

Toxic substances: Materials that are poisonous or harmful to humans, animals, or the environment, such as pesticides, acids, and certain types of chemicals.

Radioactive materials: Materials that emit ionizing radiation, such as uranium and other radioactive elements, and medical isotopes used in medical procedures.

Regulations and Laws Governing the Transport of Hazardous Materials

The transport of hazardous materials is regulated by a number of federal, state, and local laws and agencies, including the Department of Transportation (DOT), the Environmental Protection Agency (EPA), and the Occupational Safety and Health Administration (OSHA). These agencies establish standards and regulations for the packaging, labeling, handling, and transport of hazardous materials, as well as the training and certification requirements for individuals and organizations involved in the transport of these materials.

In the United States, the DOT is responsible for regulating the transport of hazardous materials by all modes of transportation, including road, rail, air, and water. The DOT has established a comprehensive set of rules and regulations known as the Hazardous Materials Regulations (HMR), which cover the transportation of hazardous materials by motor carriers, railroads, and pipelines. The HMR includes requirements for the proper packaging, labeling, and documentation of hazardous materials, as well as the training and certification of individuals involved in the transport of these materials.

The EPA is responsible for regulating the transportation of hazardous materials that pose a risk to the environment, such as hazardous waste and other materials that may be harmful to air, water, or soil. The EPA has established a number of programs and regulations to protect the environment from the potential impacts of hazardous materials, including the Resource Conservation and Recovery Act (RCRA) and the Comprehensive Environmental Response, Compensation, and Liability Act (CERCLA).

For training purposes, you can mark the ☐ symbol next to what you think is the correct answer: Once you have chosen the correct answer, use a pencil or pen to mark the ☐ symbol next to that answer.

Transportation of hazardous materials exam

1. **Which of the following is NOT a hazard class for hazardous materials?**

A. ☐ Explosives

B. ☐ Gases

C. ☐ Flammable liquids

D. ☐ Perishable goods

2. **Which of the following is NOT a hazard class of hazardous materials?**

A. ☐ Explosive

B. ☐ Flammable

C. ☐ Corrosive

D. ☐ Perishable

3. **When transporting hazardous materials, what is the maximum amount of a hazardous substance that can be placed in a single packaging?**

A. ☐ The maximum amount allowed by law

B. ☐ The maximum amount that can fit in the packaging

C. ☐ The maximum amount recommended by the manufacturer

D. ☐ None of the above

4. **What is the purpose of the placards that must be displayed on the exterior of a vehicle transporting hazardous materials?**

A. ☐ To identify the type of hazardous material being transported

B. ☐ To alert first responders to the presence of hazardous materials in the event of an emergency

C. ☐ Both A and B

D. ☐ None of the above

5. When transporting hazardous materials, which of the following is NOT required on the shipping papers?

A. ☐ The proper shipping name of the hazardous material

B. ☐ The hazard class of the hazardous material

C. ☐ The identification number of the hazardous material

D. ☐ The weight of the hazardous material

6. What is the minimum distance that a vehicle transporting hazardous materials must maintain from a hospital, school, or place of worship?

A. ☐ 500 feet

B. ☐ 1000 feet

C. ☐ 1500 feet

D. ☐ 2000 feet

7. When transporting hazardous materials, what must be done with all labels and placards when the material is transferred to another mode of transportation?

A. ☐ The labels and placards must be removed

B. ☐ The labels and placards must be covered up

C. ☐ The labels and placards must be left as is

D. ☐ The labels and placards must be replaced with new ones

8. Which of the following is NOT a requirement for the packaging of hazardous materials?

A. ☐ The packaging must be strong enough to withstand normal handling

B. ☐ The packaging must be leak-proof

C. ☐ The packaging must be able to withstand extreme temperatures

D. ☐ The packaging must be opaque

9. What is the minimum distance that a vehicle transporting hazardous materials must maintain from a stationary public transportation vehicle or a passenger terminal?

A. ☐ 500 feet

B. ☐ 1000 feet

C. ☐ 1500 feet

D. ☐ 2000 feet

10. When transporting hazardous materials, what must be done with all shipping papers if the material is transferred to another mode of transportation?

A. ☐ The shipping papers must be removed

B. ☐ The shipping papers must be covered up

C. ☐ The shipping papers must be left as is

D. ☐ The shipping papers must be replaced with new ones

11. Which of the following is NOT a requirement for the labeling of hazardous materials?

A. ☐ The label must be legible and prominently displayed

B. ☐ The label must contain the proper shipping name of the hazardous material

C. ☐ The label must contain the hazard class of the hazardous material

D. ☐ The label must be in a foreign language

12. Which of the following is not a requirement for transporting hazardous materials by ground?

A. ☐ The materials must be properly labeled and packaged.

B. ☐ The driver must have a special endorsement on their commercial driver's license.

C. ☐ The vehicle must be equipped with special safety equipment.

D. ☐ The materials must be transported in a fully enclosed vehicle.

13. In the event of an accident involving hazardous materials, which of the following should the driver do first?

A. ☐ Notify emergency services

B. ☐ Evacuate the area

C. ☐ Attempt to contain the spill

D. ☐ Secure the vehicle

14. Which of the following is not required to be included on a hazardous materials shipping paper?

A. ☐ The hazardous materials' proper shipping name

B. ☐ The hazard class of the materials

C. ☐ The identification number for the materials

D. ☐ The weight of the package

15. How often must a driver of a vehicle transporting hazardous materials complete a hazardous materials refresher training course?

A. ☐ Every year

B. ☐ Every two years

C. ☐ Every three years

D. ☐ Every four years

Correct answers for transportation of hazardous materials exam

1.   **D.** Perishable goods

2.   **D.** Perishable is NOT a hazard class of hazardous materials. The hazard classes of hazardous materials are Explosive, Flammable, Corrosive, and others as defined by regulatory agencies such as the Department of Transportation (DOT) in the United States.

3.   **C.** The maximum amount of a hazardous substance that can be placed in a single packaging is the maximum amount recommended by the manufacturer, which is determined based on the hazardous characteristics of the substance and the requirements of the applicable regulations.

4.   **C.** Placards displayed on the exterior of a vehicle transporting hazardous materials serve to identify the type of hazardous material being transported and alert first responders to the presence of hazardous materials in the event of an emergency.

5.   **D.** The weight of the hazardous material is NOT required on the shipping papers for the transportation of hazardous materials. The shipping papers must include the proper shipping name of the hazardous material, the hazard class of the hazardous material, and the identification number of the hazardous material.

6.   **B.** The minimum distance that a vehicle transporting hazardous materials must maintain from a hospital, school, or place of worship is 1000 feet.

7.   **C.** When the hazardous material is transferred to another mode of transportation, the labels and placards must be left as is and remain visible.

8.   **D.** The packaging of hazardous materials does NOT need to be opaque. It must be strong enough to withstand normal handling, leak-proof, and able to withstand extreme temperatures as required by regulatory agencies such as the DOT.

9.   **B.** The minimum distance that a vehicle transporting hazardous materials must maintain from a stationary public transportation vehicle or a passenger terminal is 1000 feet.

10.   **C.** When the hazardous material is transferred to another mode of transportation, the shipping papers must be left as is and remain with the material.

11.   **D.** The label for hazardous materials does NOT need to be in a foreign language. It must be legible and prominently displayed, and contain the proper shipping name and hazard class of the hazardous material.

12.   **B.** The driver must have a special endorsement on their commercial driver's license.

13. **A.** The driver should first notify emergency services in the event of an accident involving hazardous materials.

14. **D.** The weight of the package is not required to be included on a hazardous materials shipping paper.

15. **B.** Drivers of vehicles transporting hazardous materials must complete a hazardous materials refresher training course every two years.

Transportation of hazardous materials exam 2

1. **What is the maximum amount of hazardous materials that can be transported in a single package without requiring additional hazard placards on the vehicle?**

   A. ☐ 1,001 pounds

   B. ☐ 1,500 pounds

   C. ☐ 2,000 pounds

   D. ☐ 2,500 pounds

2. **When transporting hazardous materials, the driver must have immediate access to which of the following documents?**

   A. ☐ The hazardous materials shipping paper

   B. ☐ The emergency response guidebook

   C. ☐ The driver's logbook

   D. ☐ All of the above

3. **When transporting hazardous materials, the driver must do which of the following at all times?**

   A. ☐ Follow all traffic laws and regulations

   B. ☐ Keep the materials properly labeled and packaged

   C. ☐ Wear personal protective equipment

   D. ☐ All of the above

4. **In the event of a hazardous materials spill, which of the following should the driver do first?**

   A. ☐ Notify emergency services

   B. ☐ Evacuate the area

   C. ☐ Attempt to contain the spill

   D. ☐ Secure the vehicle

5. Which of the following is NOT a required placard for the transportation of hazardous materials?

A. ☐ Flammable gas

B. ☐Poisonous gas

C. ☐ Compressed gas

D. ☐ Explosive

6. Under what circumstances is it acceptable to transport hazardous materials in a passenger vehicle?

A. ☐ The vehicle has a special permit

B. ☐ The hazardous materials are in limited quantities

C. ☐ The hazardous materials are properly labeled and packaged

D. ☐ None of the above

7. What is the minimum distance that a vehicle transporting hazardous materials must maintain from a school bus when driving on a two-lane road?

A. ☐ 500 feet

B. ☐ 1000 feet

C. ☐ 1500 feet

D. ☐ 2000 feet

8. When transporting hazardous materials, what is the maximum speed that a vehicle can travel on a highway?

A. ☐ 55 mph

B. ☐ 60 mph

C. ☐ 65 mph

D. ☐ The maximum speed limit for the roadway

9. What is the minimum number of hazmat employees that must be trained to handle hazardous materials?

A. ☐ One

B. ☐ Two

C. ☐ Three

D. ☐ Four

10. In the event of a hazardous materials spill, what should be the first action taken?

A. ☐ Notify the appropriate authorities

B. ☐ Evacuate the area

C. ☐ Contain the spill

D. ☐ Clean up the spill

11. What is the purpose of the Emergency Response Guidebook (ERG)?

A. ☐ To provide information on the proper shipping names and identification numbers for hazardous materials

B. ☐ To outline the proper procedures for responding to a hazardous materials incident

C. ☐ To list the proper placarding requirements for each hazard class

D. ☐ To outline the requirements for packaging and labeling hazardous materials

12. When transporting hazardous materials, what is the maximum amount of a single hazardous material that can be placed in one vehicle?

A. ☐ 50 pounds

B. ☐ 100 pounds

C. ☐ 500 pounds

D. ☐ 1,000 pounds

13. What is the maximum amount of hazardous materials that can be transported in a single vehicle without requiring placards?

    A. ☐ 25 kg

    B. ☐ 100 kg

    C. ☐ 500 kg

    D. ☐ 1000 kg

14. When transporting hazardous materials, what must be done with any waste materials generated during the transportation process?

    A. ☐ Disposed of in a designated waste disposal facility

    B. ☐ Left at the delivery location

    C. ☐ Kept on the vehicle until the next delivery

    D. ☐ Disposed of in a designated waste disposal facility or left at the delivery location, depending on the material

15. What is the primary hazard associated with transporting Class 3 Flammable Liquids?

    A. ☐ Explosive

    B. ☐ Corrosive

    C. ☐ Toxic

    D. ☐ Radioactive

Correct answers for transportation of hazardous materials exam 2

1. **C.** The maximum amount of hazardous materials that can be transported in a single package without requiring additional hazard placards on the vehicle is 2,000 pounds.

2. **D.** The driver must have immediate access to the hazardous materials shipping paper, the emergency response guidebook, and the driver's logbook at all times when transporting hazardous materials.

3. **D.** When transporting hazardous materials, the driver must follow all traffic laws and regulations, keep the materials properly labeled and packaged, and wear personal protective equipment at all times.

4. **A.** In the event of a hazardous materials spill, the driver should first notify emergency services.

5. **D.** Explosive is not a required placard for the transportation of hazardous materials. The required placards are: flammable gas, non-flammable gas, poisonous gas, flammable liquid, flammable solid, spontaneous combustible, dangerous when wet, oxidizer, poison, radioactive, corrosive, and inhalation hazard.

6. **D.** It is not acceptable to transport hazardous materials in a passenger vehicle under any circumstances. Hazardous materials must be transported in a vehicle that is specifically designed and equipped to handle them safely.

7. **B.** The minimum distance that a vehicle transporting hazardous materials must maintain from a school bus when driving on a two-lane road is 1000 feet.

8. **A.** When transporting hazardous materials, the maximum speed that a vehicle can travel on a highway is 55 mph.

9. **A.** The minimum number of hazmat employees that must be trained to handle hazardous materials is one.

10. **A.** The first action to be taken in the event of a hazardous materials spill is to notify the appropriate authorities.

11. **B.** To outline the proper procedures for responding to a hazardous materials incident

12. **C.** 500 pounds

13. **C.** The maximum amount of hazardous materials that can be transported in a single vehicle without requiring placards is 500 kg.

14. D. Any waste materials generated during the transportation of hazardous materials must be disposed of in a designated waste disposal facility or left at the delivery location, depending on the material.

15. A. The primary hazard associated with transporting Class 3 Flammable Liquids is explosive.

Transportation of hazardous materials exam 3

1. **What is the purpose of the Hazardous Materials Table (HMT)?**

A. ☐ To provide information on the proper shipping names and identification numbers for hazardous materials

B. ☐ To list the proper placarding requirements for each hazard class

C. ☐ To outline the requirements for packaging and labeling hazardous materials

D. ☐ All of the above

2. **How many placards are required to be displayed on a vehicle transporting hazardous materials in quantities that require placarding?**

A. ☐ One

B. ☐ Two

C. ☐ Three

D. ☐ Four

3. **Which of the following is NOT a requirement for a person transporting hazardous materials?**

A. ☐ Obtain a hazardous materials endorsement on their commercial driver's license

B. ☐ Have completed a training program on the safe transportation of hazardous materials

C. ☐ Wear protective clothing while driving

D. ☐ Have a valid medical certificate

4. **What is the minimum distance a vehicle transporting hazardous materials must be from a building or place where people gather during loading and unloading?**

A. ☐ 25 feet

B. ☐ 50 feet

C. ☐ 75 feet

D. ☐ 100 feet

5. **What must be included in the shipping papers for a hazardous material shipment?**

A. ☐ The name and address of the consignee

B. ☐ The proper shipping name of the hazardous material

C. ☐ The UN or NA number of the hazardous material

D. ☐ All of the above

6. **When driving a vehicle transporting hazardous materials, what should you do if you are involved in an accident?**

A. ☐ Evacuate the area immediately

B. ☐ Secure the hazardous material and try to prevent it from leaking

C. ☐ Contact the police and your supervisor

D. ☐ All of the above

7. **How should hazardous materials spills be cleaned up?**

A. ☐ Using a broom and dustpan

B. ☐ Using a vacuum cleaner

C. ☐ Using appropriate personal protective equipment and following the guidelines outlined in the Material Safety Data Sheet (MSDS)

D. ☐ Using a garden hose

8. **Which of the following is NOT a requirement for transporting hazardous materials?**

A. ☐ The materials must be properly labeled and placarded

B. ☐ The driver must have a hazardous materials endorsement on their commercial driver's license

C. ☐ The materials must be stored in a secure and properly labeled container

D. ☐ The vehicle must be equipped with a fire extinguisher

9. When transporting hazardous materials, what is the maximum amount of a single hazardous material that can be placed in one container?

A. ☐ 50 pounds

B. ☐ 100 pounds

C. ☐ 500 pounds

D. ☐ 1,000 pounds

10. What is the minimum distance that must be maintained between a vehicle transporting hazardous materials and other vehicles?

A. ☐ 50 feet

B. ☐ 100 feet

C. ☐ 250 feet

D. ☐ 500 feet

11. What is the proper method for storing hazardous materials in a vehicle?

A. ☐ Loose in the trunk

B. ☐ In a cardboard box on the passenger seat

C. ☐ In a properly labeled and secured container

D. ☐ In the bed of a pickup truck

12. When transporting hazardous materials, what must be displayed on the exterior of the vehicle?

A. ☐ A hazardous materials placard

B. ☐ A hazardous materials sticker

C. ☐ A hazardous materials decal

D. ☐ A hazardous materials sign

13. What is the primary concern when transporting hazardous materials?

A. ☐ Ensuring the materials are delivered on time

B. ☐ Protecting the environment

C. ☐ Protecting the public from accidental release or exposure to the materials

D. ☐ Protecting the materials from damage

14. Who is responsible for ensuring that hazardous materials are properly packaged and labeled?

A. ☐ The driver

B. ☐ The shipper

C. ☐ The carrier

D. ☐ The receiver

15. What is the first step in responding to a hazardous materials incident?

A. ☐ Evacuating the area

B. ☐ Notifying emergency response personnel

C. ☐ Containing the release

D. ☐ Identifying the hazardous material involved

Correct answers for transportation of hazardous materials exam 3

1. **D.** All of the above

2. **A.** Only one placard is required to be displayed on a vehicle transporting hazardous materials in quantities that require placarding.

3. **D.** A valid medical certificate is NOT a requirement for a person transporting hazardous materials. Obtaining a hazardous materials endorsement on their commercial driver's license and completing a training program on the safe transportation of hazardous materials are both required.

4. **B.** The minimum distance a vehicle transporting hazardous materials must be from a building or place where people gather during loading and unloading is 50 feet.

5. **D.** Shipping papers for a hazardous material shipment must include the name and address of the consignee, the proper shipping name of the hazardous material, and the UN or NA number of the hazardous material.

6. **D.** If you are involved in an accident while driving a vehicle transporting hazardous materials, you should evacuate the area immediately, secure the hazardous material and try to prevent it from leaking, and contact the police and your supervisor.

7. **C.** Using appropriate personal protective equipment and following the guidelines outlined in the Material Safety Data Sheet (MSDS)

8. **D.** The vehicle must be equipped with a fire extinguisher

9. **C.** 500 pounds

10. **C.** 250 feet

11. **C.** In a properly labeled and secured container

12. **A.** A hazardous materials placard

13. **C.** Protecting the public from accidental release or exposure to the materials

14. **B.** The shipper

15. **D.** Identifying the hazardous material involved

Transportation of hazardous materials exam 4

1. **What is the primary hazard associated with transporting Class 8 Corrosive Materials?**

   A. ☐ Explosive

   B. ☐ Flammable

   C. ☐ Toxic

   D. ☐ Corrosive

2. **What should you do if you suspect that the hazardous material you are transporting has been damaged or leaking?**

   A. ☐ Continue driving to the destination

   B. ☐ Stop the vehicle and secure the hazardous material

   C. ☐ Evacuate the area immediately

   D. ☐ Contact the shipper or consignee

3. **When transporting hazardous materials, which of the following must be displayed on the vehicle?**

   A. ☐ A red triangle with a white border

   B. ☐ A white square with a red border

   C. ☐ A white diamond with a black border

   D. ☐ A black square with a white border

4. **When transporting hazardous materials, which of the following is required for the driver to possess?**

   A. ☐ A commercial driver's license

   B. ☐ A hazardous materials endorsement

   C. ☐ Both A and B

   D. ☐ None of the above

5. **When transporting hazardous materials, which of the following is required for the vehicle to be equipped with?**

A. ☐ Fire extinguishers

B. ☐ Reflective triangles

C. ☐ Flashing lights

D. ☐ All of the above

6. **When transporting hazardous materials, which of the following must be followed when loading and unloading the materials?**

A. ☐ Use proper lifting techniques

B. ☐ Follow all applicable OSHA regulations

C. ☐ Both A and B

D. ☐ None of the above

7. **When transporting hazardous materials, which of the following is required for the vehicle to be marked with?**

A. ☐ The UN number of the hazardous material being transported

B. ☐ The placard for the hazardous material being transported

C. ☐ Both A and B

D. ☐ None of the above

8. **When transporting hazardous materials, which of the following must be followed when driving through tunnels or under bridges?**

A. ☐ Check the height of the tunnel or bridge before entering

B. ☐ Notify local authorities if the hazardous material cannot pass through the tunnel or bridge

C. ☐ Both A and B

D. ☐ None of the above

9. When transporting hazardous materials, which of the following must be followed in the event of a spill or leak?

A. ☐ Contain the spill or leak as much as possible

B. ☐ Evacuate the area immediately

C. ☐ Notify local authorities

D. ☐ All of the above

10. When transporting hazardous materials, which of the following must be followed when driving through a residential area?

A. ☐ Drive slowly and cautiously

B. ☐ Use flashing lights and/or a siren to alert pedestrians and other vehicles

C. ☐ Both A and B

D. ☐ None of the above

11. What is the primary hazard associated with transporting hazardous materials?

A. ☐ Explosion

B. ☐ Fire

C. ☐ Spillage

D. ☐ Corrosion

12. What should you do if you are involved in an accident while transporting hazardous materials?

A. ☐ Exit the vehicle as quickly as possible

B. ☐ Stay inside the vehicle and wait for help

C. ☐ Attempt to contain the spillage

D. ☐ All of the above

13. How should you label a container of hazardous materials?

A. ☐ With the name of the hazardous material

B. ☐ With the UN number of the hazardous material

C. ☐ With the hazard class of the hazardous material

D. ☐ All of the above

14. What is the primary function of placards on a vehicle transporting hazardous materials?

A. ☐ To identify the hazardous material being transported

B. ☐ To provide emergency response information

C. ☐ To indicate the proper loading and unloading procedures

D. ☐ All of the above

15. What should you do if you suspect that a hazardous material has been released in the vicinity of your vehicle?

A. ☐ Evacuate the area immediately

B. ☐ Stay inside the vehicle and wait for help

C. ☐ Attempt to contain the spillage

D. ☐ All of the above

Correct answers for transportation of hazardous materials exam 4

1. **D.** The primary hazard associated with transporting Class 8 Corrosive Materials is corrosive.

2. **B.** If you suspect that the hazardous material you are transporting has been damaged or leaking, you should stop the vehicle and secure the hazardous material.

3. **C.** A white diamond with a black border

4. **C.** Both A and B

5. **D.** All of the above

6. **C.** Both A and B

7. **C.** Both A and B

8. **C.** Both A and B

9. **D.** All of the above

10. **A.** Drive slowly and cautiously

11. **D.** Corrosion

12. **D.** All of the above

13. **D.** All of the above

14. **D.** All of the above

15. **D.** All of the above

Transportation of hazardous materials exam 5

1. **What is the primary goal of the Hazardous Materials Regulations (HMR)?**

A. ☐ To prevent accidents and incidents involving hazardous materials

B. ☐ To ensure that hazardous materials are properly packaged and labeled

C. ☐ To regulate the transportation of hazardous materials

D. ☐ To protect the environment from the effects of hazardous materials

2. **Which of the following is NOT a requirement for transporting hazardous materials by air?**

A. ☐ The material must be properly packaged and labeled

B. ☐ The aircraft must be properly marked and placarded

C. ☐ The shipper must have a permit from the airline

D. ☐ The material must be approved for transportation by the airline

3. **When transporting hazardous materials, which of the following must be included on the shipping papers?**

A. ☐ The proper shipping name of the hazardous material

B. ☐ The hazard class of the material

C. ☐ The identification number of the hazardous material

D. ☐ All of the above

4. **Who is responsible for ensuring that hazardous materials are properly packaged and labeled before transportation?**

A. ☐ The transportation company

B. ☐ The hazardous materials shipper

C. ☐ The driver of the vehicle

D. ☐ The government regulatory agency

5. **When transporting hazardous materials, what is the maximum amount of a hazardous material that may be shipped on a single package?**

A. ☐ The maximum allowed by the transportation company

B. ☐ The amount that can fit in the vehicle

C. ☐ The amount necessary for the trip

D. ☐ None, there is no maximum amount for a single package

6. **In the event of an accident involving hazardous materials, who is responsible for taking the necessary emergency response actions?**

A. ☐ The transportation company

B. ☐ The hazardous materials shipper

C. ☐ The driver of the vehicle

D. ☐ The government regulatory agency

7. **Which of the following is NOT a requirement for shipping hazardous materials by rail?**

A. ☐ The material must be properly packaged and labeled

B. ☐ The railcar must be properly marked and placarded

C. ☐ The shipper must have a permit from the rail company

D. ☐ The material must be approved for transportation by the rail company

8. **What should you do if you are driving a vehicle that is leaking hazardous material?**

A. ☐ Stop the vehicle as soon as it is safe to do so

B. ☐ Continue driving until you reach your destination

C. ☐ Attempt to repair the leak yourself

D. ☐ All of the above

9. **When transporting hazardous materials, which of the following is NOT required to be included on the shipping papers?**

A. ☐ The proper shipping name of the hazardous material

B. ☐ The hazard class of the material

C. ☐ The identification number of the hazardous material

D. ☐ The weight of the package

10. **Which of the following is NOT a requirement for shipping hazardous materials by highway?**

A. ☐ The material must be properly packaged and labeled

B. ☐ The vehicle must be properly marked and placarded

C. ☐ The shipper must have a permit from the highway authority

D. ☐ The material must be approved for transportation by the highway authority

11. **Which of the following is NOT a hazard class for the transportation of hazardous materials?**

A. ☐ Explosives

B. ☐ Radioactive materials

C. ☐ Flammable liquids

D. ☐ Fresh produce

12. **When transporting hazardous materials, which of the following is required to be displayed on the exterior of the vehicle?**

A. ☐ The UN number of the hazardous material

B. ☐ The name of the driver

C. ☐ The weight of the load

D. ☐ The vehicle's license plate number

13. What is the maximum amount of hazardous material that may be shipped on a passenger aircraft?

A. ☐ The maximum allowed by the airline

B. ☐ The amount that can fit in the cargo hold

C. ☐ The amount necessary for the trip

D. ☐ None, hazardous materials are not allowed on passenger aircraft

14. Which of the following is NOT a requirement for shipping hazardous materials by sea?

A. ☐ The material must be properly packaged and labeled

B. ☐ The vessel must be properly marked and placarded

C. ☐ The shipper must have a permit from the shipping company

D. ☐ The material must be approved for transportation by the shipping company

15. What is the purpose of the emergency response telephone number on a hazardous materials shipping label?

A. ☐ To provide emergency medical treatment information

B. ☐ To provide information about the hazardous material being shipped

C. ☐ To provide the telephone number of the person responsible for the shipment

D. ☐ To provide the telephone number for emergency responders to call in case of an accident involving the hazardous material

Correct answers for transportation of hazardous materials exam 5

1. **A** The primary goal of the Hazardous Materials Regulations (HMR) is to prevent accidents and incidents involving hazardous materials.

2. **D** The material must be approved for transportation by the airline is not a requirement for transporting hazardous materials by air.

3. **D** All of the above must be included on the shipping papers when transporting hazardous materials.

4. **B.** The hazardous materials shipper is responsible for ensuring that hazardous materials are properly packaged and labeled before transportation.

5. **C.** The maximum amount of hazardous material that may be shipped on a single package is the amount necessary for the trip.

6. **D.** The government regulatory agency is responsible for taking the necessary emergency response actions in the event of an accident involving hazardous materials.

7. **D.** The material must be approved for transportation by the rail company is not a requirement for shipping hazardous materials by rail.

8. **A.** Stop the vehicle as soon as it is safe to do so

9. **D.** The weight of the package is not required to be included on the shipping papers when transporting hazardous materials.

10. **D.** The material must be approved for transportation by the highway authority is not a requirement for shipping hazardous materials by highway.

11. **D.** Fresh produce is not a hazard class for the transportation of hazardous materials.

12. **A.** The UN number of the hazardous material must be displayed on the exterior of the vehicle when transporting hazardous materials.

13. **D.** Hazardous materials are not allowed on passenger aircraft.

14. **D.** The material must be approved for transportation by the shipping company is not a requirement for shipping hazardous materials by sea.

15. **D.** The emergency response telephone number on a hazardous materials shipping label is for emergency responders to call in case of an accident involving the hazardous material.

Vehicle registration and insurance

As a new driver in California, it is important to understand the process of registering and insuring your vehicle. Not only is it a legal requirement, but it also protects you and others on the road in the event of an accident.

In this chapter, we will cover the basics of vehicle registration and insurance in California, including the necessary documents and fees, as well as the process for renewing your registration and insurance. We will also discuss the importance of maintaining proof of insurance, as well as the consequences of driving without proper coverage.

In addition to understanding the basics of vehicle registration and insurance, it is also important to be well-prepared for your driving tests. In this chapter, we will provide tips and resources for practicing and preparing for the California driving test, including the knowledge test and the behind-the-wheel test.

We will also cover the different types of driving tests available in California, including the regular driving test, the senior driving test, and the driving test for drivers with disabilities.

By the end of this chapter, you should have a thorough understanding of the process of registering and insuring your vehicle in California, as well as the resources and tips available to help you prepare for and pass your driving tests.

For training purposes, you can mark the ☐ symbol next to what you think is the correct answer: Once you have chosen the correct answer, use a pencil or pen to mark the ☐ symbol next to that answer.

So let's get started!

Vehicle registration and insurance exam

1. **What is the minimum liability insurance required by law in the state of California?**

    A. ☐ $25,000 per person, $50,000 per accident

    B. ☐ $15,000 per person, $30,000 per accident

    C. ☐ $50,000 per person, $100,000 per accident

    D. ☐ $100,000 per person, $300,000 per accident

2. **What is the penalty for driving without a valid driver's license in the state of Texas?**

    A. ☐ $100 fine

    B. ☐ 6 months in jail

    C. ☐ Suspension of driving privileges

    D. ☐ All of the above

3. **When must you renew your vehicle registration in the state of New York?**

    A. ☐ Every 6 months

    B. ☐ Every year

    C. ☐ Every 2 years

    D. ☐ Every 5 years

4. **What is the minimum age to obtain a driver's license in the state of Florida?**

    A. ☐ 16 years old

    B. ☐ 18 years old

    C. ☐ 21 years old

    D. ☐ 25 years old

5. **In order to renew your vehicle registration, which of the following documents must you have?**

A. ☐ Proof of insurance

B. ☐ Vehicle title

C. ☐ Vehicle inspection certificate

D. ☐ All of the above

6. **Who is responsible for maintaining proof of insurance in the state of Illinois?**

A. ☐ The insurance company

B. ☐ The vehicle owner

C. ☐ The state Department of Motor Vehicles

D. ☐ The police

7. **What is the penalty for driving with a suspended license in the state of Arizona?**

A. ☐ $500 fine

B. ☐ 6 months in jail

C. ☐ Suspension of driving privileges

D. ☐ All of the above

8. **When must you renew your vehicle registration in the state of Georgia?**

A. ☐ Every 6 months

B. ☐ Every year

C. ☐ Every 2 years

D. ☐ Every 5 years

9. What is the minimum age to obtain a driver's license in the state of Michigan?

A. ☐ 16 years old

B. ☐ 18 years old

C. ☐ 21 years old

D. ☐ 25 years old

10. How often must you renew your vehicle inspection sticker in the state of New Jersey?

A. ☐ Every 6 months

B. ☐ Every year

C. ☐ Every 2 years

D. ☐ Every 5 years

11. What is the minimum age to obtain a driver's license in the state of California?

A. ☐ 15 years old

B. ☐ 16 years old

C. ☐ 18 years old

D. ☐ 21 years old

12. When must you renew your vehicle registration in the state of Texas?

A. ☐ Every 6 months

B. ☐ Every year

C. ☐ Every 2 years

D. ☐ Every 5 years

13. What is the penalty for driving without a valid driver's license in the state of New York?

A. ☐ $100 fine

B. ☐ 6 months in jail

C. ☐ Suspension of driving privileges

D. ☐ All of the above

14. What is the minimum liability insurance required by law in the state of Florida?

A. ☐ $25,000 per person, $50,000 per accident

B. ☐ $15,000 per person, $30,000 per accident

C. ☐ $50,000 per person, $100,000 per accident

D. ☐ $100,000 per person, $300,000 per accident

15. How often must you renew your vehicle inspection sticker in the state of Massachusetts?

A. ☐ Every 6 months

B. ☐ Every year

C. ☐ Every 2 years

D. ☐ Every 5 years

Correct answers for vehicle registration and insurance exam

1. **C.** $50,000 per person, $100,000 per accident
2. **D.** All of the above
3. **B.** Every year
4. **A.** 16 years old
5. **B.** Every year
6. **B.** The vehicle owner
7. **D.** All of the above
8. **C.** Every 2 years
9. **A.** 16 years old
10. **A.** Every 6 months
11. **B.** 16 years old
12. **B.** Every year
13. **D.** All of the above
14. **C.** $50,000 per person, $100,000 per accident
15. **A.** Every 6 months

Vehicle registration and insurance exam 2

1. **What is the minimum age to obtain a driver's license in the state of Ohio?**

   A. ☐ 15 years old

   B. ☐ 16 years old

   C. ☐ 18 years old

   D. ☐ 21 years old

2. **When must you renew your vehicle registration in the state of Pennsylvania?**

   A. ☐ Every 6 months

   B. ☐ Every year

   C. ☐ Every 2 years

   D. ☐ Every 5 years

3. **What is the penalty for driving without a valid driver's license in the state of Virginia?**

   A. ☐ $100 fine

   B. ☐ 6 months in jail

   C. ☐ Suspension of driving privileges

   D. ☐ All of the above

4. **What is the minimum liability insurance required by law in the state of North Carolina?**

   A. ☐ $25,000 per person, $50,000 per accident

   B. ☐ $15,000 per person, $30,000 per accident

   C. ☐ $50,000 per person, $100,000 per accident

   D. ☐ $100,000 per person, $300,000 per accident

5. How often must you renew your vehicle inspection sticker in the state of New Hampshire?

A. ☐ Every 6 months

B. ☐ Every year

C. ☐ Every 2 years

D. ☐ Every 5 years

6. Who is responsible for maintaining proof of insurance in the state of Maryland?

A. ☐ The insurance company

B. ☐ The vehicle owner

C. ☐ The state Department of Motor Vehicles

D. ☐ The police

7. What is the penalty for driving with a suspended license in the state of West Virginia?

A. ☐ $500 fine

B. ☐ 6 months in jail

C. ☐ Suspension of driving privileges

D. ☐ All of the above

8. When must you renew your vehicle registration in the state of Vermont?

A. ☐ Every 6 months

B. ☐ Every year

C. ☐ Every 2 years

D. ☐ Every 5 years

9. What is the minimum age to obtain a driver's license in the state of Maine?

A. ☐ 16 years old

B. ☐ 18 years old

C. ☐ 21 years old

D. ☐ 25 years old

10. How often must you renew your vehicle inspection sticker in the state of Rhode Island?

A. ☐ Every 6 months

B. ☐ Every year

C. ☐ Every 2 years

D. ☐ Every 5 years

11. What is the minimum age to obtain a driver's license in the state of Alaska?

A. ☐ 15 years old

B. ☐ 16 years old

C. ☐ 18 years old

D. ☐ 21 years old

12. When must you renew your vehicle registration in the state of Arkansas?

A. ☐ Every 6 months

B. ☐ Every year

C. ☐ Every 2 years

D. ☐ Every 5 years

13. What is the penalty for driving without a valid driver's license in the state of Colorado?

A. ☐ $100 fine

B. ☐ 6 months in jail

C. ☐ Suspension of driving privileges

D. ☐ All of the above

14. What is the minimum liability insurance required by law in the state of Delaware?

A. ☐ $25,000 per person, $50,000 per accident

B. ☐ $15,000 per person, $30,000 per accident

C. ☐ $50,000 per person, $100,000 per accident

D. ☐ $100,000 per person, $300,000 per accident

15. How often must you renew your vehicle inspection sticker in the state of Hawaii?

A. ☐ Every 6 months

B. ☐ Every year

C. ☐ Every 2 years

D. ☐ Every 5 years

Correct answers for vehicle registration and insurance exam 2

1. **B.** 16 years old
2. **B.** Every year
3. **D.** All of the above
4. **C.** $50,000 per person, $100,000 per accident
5. **A.** Every 6 months
6. **B.** The vehicle owner
7. **D.** All of the above
8. **B.** Every year
9. **A.** 16 years old
10. **A.** Every 6 months
11. **B.** 16 years old
12. **B.** Every year
13. **D.** All of the above
14. **C.** $50,000 per person, $100,000 per accident
15. **A.** Every 6 months

Vehicle registration and insurance exam 3

1. **What is the minimum age to obtain a driver's license in the state of Idaho?**

   A. ☐ 15 years old
   B. ☐ 16 years old
   C. ☐ 18 years old
   D. ☐ 21 years old

2. **When must you renew your vehicle registration in the state of Iowa?**

   A. ☐ Every 6 months
   B. ☐ Every year
   C. ☐ Every 2 years
   D. ☐ Every 5 years

3. **What is the penalty for driving without a valid driver's license in the state of Kansas?**

   A. ☐ $100 fine
   B. ☐ 6 months in jail
   C. ☐ Suspension of driving privileges
   D. ☐ All of the above

4. **What is the minimum liability insurance required by law in the state of Kentucky?**

   A. ☐ $25,000 per person, $50,000 per accident
   B. ☐ $15,000 per person, $30,000 per accident
   C. ☐ $50,000 per person, $100,000 per accident
   D. ☐ $100,000 per person, $300,000 per accident

5. How often must you renew your vehicle inspection sticker in the state of Louisiana?

A. ☐ Every 6 months

B. ☐ Every year

C. ☐ Every 2 years

D. ☐ Every 5 years

6. Who is responsible for maintaining proof of insurance in the state of Mississippi?

A. ☐ The insurance company

B. ☐ The vehicle owner

C. ☐ The state Department of Motor Vehicles

D. ☐ The police

7. What is the penalty for driving with a suspended license in the state of Missouri?

A. ☐ $500 fine

B. ☐ 6 months in jail

C. ☐ Suspension of driving privileges

D. ☐ All of the above

8. When must you renew your vehicle registration in the state of Montana?

A. ☐ Every 6 months

B. ☐ Every year

C. ☐ Every 2 years

D. ☐ Every 5 years

9. What is the minimum age to obtain a driver's license in the state of Nebraska?

A. ☐ 16 years old

B. ☐ 18 years old

C. ☐ 21 years old

D. ☐ 25 years old

10. How often must you renew your vehicle inspection sticker in the state of Nevada?

A. ☐ Every 6 months

B. ☐ Every year

C. ☐ Every 2 years

D. ☐ Every 5 years

11. What is the minimum age to obtain a driver's license in the state of New Mexico?

A. ☐ 15 years old

B. ☐ 16 years old

C. ☐ 18 years old

D. ☐ 21 years old

12. When must you renew your vehicle registration in the state of North Dakota?

A. ☐ Every 6 months

B. ☐ Every year

C. ☐ Every 2 years

D. ☐ Every 5 years

13. What is the penalty for driving without a valid driver's license in the state of Oklahoma?

A. ☐ $100 fine

B. ☐ 6 months in jail

C. ☐ Suspension of driving privileges

D. ☐ All of the above

14. What is the minimum liability insurance required by law in the state of Oregon?

A. ☐ $25,000 per person, $50,000 per accident

B. ☐ $15,000 per person, $30,000 per accident

C. ☐ $50,000 per person, $100,000 per accident

D. ☐ $100,000 per person, $300,000 per accident

15. How often must you renew your vehicle inspection sticker in the state of South Dakota?

A. ☐ Every 6 months

B. ☐ Every year

C. ☐ Every 2 years

D. ☐ Every 5 years

Correct answers for vehicle registration and insurance exam 3

1. **B.** 16 years old
2. **B.** Every year
3. **D.** All of the above
4. **C.** $50,000 per person, $100,000 per accident
5. **A.** Every 6 months
6. **B.** The vehicle owner
7. **D.** All of the above
8. **B.** Every year
9. **A.** 16 years old
10. **A.** Every 6 months
11. **B.** 16 years old
12. **B.** Every year
13. **D.** All of the above
14. **C.** $50,000 per person, $100,000 per accident
15. **A.** Every 6 months

Vehicle registration and insurance exam 4

1. **If you are caught driving without insurance, what is the maximum fine you could face?**

A. ☐ $500

B. ☐ $1,000

C. ☐ $2,500

D. ☐ $5,000

2. **Which of the following is NOT typically covered by a basic car insurance policy?**

A. ☐ Liability for damages to other vehicles or property

B. ☐ Medical expenses for you and your passengers

C. ☐ Damage to your own vehicle

D. ☐ Rental car expenses

3. **If you have a loan on your vehicle, your lender will likely require you to carry which type of car insurance coverage?**

A. ☐ Collision

B. ☐ Comprehensive

C. ☐ Liability

D. ☐ Uninsured motorist

4. **If you are involved in a hit-and-run accident, what should you do?**

A. ☐ Leave the scene of the accident

B. ☐ Call the police and report the incident

C. ☐ Exchange insurance information with the other driver

D. ☐ All of the above

5. **How often do you need to renew your vehicle registration?**

A. ☐ Every year

B. ☐ Every two years

C. ☐ Every three years

D. ☐ It depends on the state you live in

6. **If you are caught driving without a valid driver's license, what could happen?**

A. ☐ You could be arrested and taken to jail

B. ☐ Your vehicle could be impounded

C. ☐ You could be fined

D. ☐ All of the above

7. **If you are involved in a car accident and you are at fault, your insurance company will likely do which of the following?**

A. ☐ Cover the damages to the other driver's vehicle

B. ☐ Pay for any medical expenses incurred by the other driver

C. ☐ Pay for damages to your own vehicle

D. ☐ All of the above

8. **If you are involved in a car accident and the other driver does not have insurance, what should you do?**

A. ☐ File a claim with your insurance company

B. ☐ Sue the other driver for damages

C. ☐ Pay for the damages out of pocket

D. ☐ Report the accident to the police

9. **What is the minimum level of liability insurance required by law in most states?**

A. ☐ $10,000

B. ☐ $25,000

C. ☐ $50,000

D. ☐ $100,000

10. **What is the main purpose of having car insurance?**

A. ☐ To cover damages to your own vehicle

B. ☐ To cover medical expenses for you and your passengers

C. ☐ To protect you financially in the event of an accident

D. ☐ To lower your monthly car payments

11. **What type of insurance covers damages to your own vehicle that are not caused by a collision?**

A. ☐ Liability insurance

B. ☐ Collision insurance

C. ☐ Comprehensive insurance

D. ☐ Personal injury protection

12. **If you are involved in an accident and it is determined to be your fault, which type of insurance would cover damages to the other party's vehicle?**

A. ☐ Liability insurance

B. ☐ Collision insurance

C. ☐ Comprehensive insurance

D. ☐ Personal injury protection

13. **If you have a loan or lease on your vehicle, your lender may require you to carry which type of insurance?**

A. ☐ The vehicle is being driven for commercial purposes

B. ☐ Collision insurance

C. ☐ Comprehensive insurance

D. ☐ GAP insurance

14. **If you are involved in an accident and the other party's damages exceed your liability coverage limits, what can happen?**

A. ☐ The other party's insurance company will cover the remaining damages

B. ☐ You will have to pay the remaining damages out of pocket

C. ☐ Your insurance company will cover the remaining damages

D. ☐ You will not be held financially responsible for the remaining damages

15. **If you lend your car to a friend and they get into an accident, what type of insurance would cover damages to the other party's vehicle?**

A. ☐ Your liability insurance

B. ☐ our collision insurance

C. ☐ Your comprehensive insurance

D. ☐ Your friend's insurance

Correct answers for vehicle registration and insurance exam 4

1. **C.** $2,500
2. **D.** Rental car expenses
3. **A.** Collision
4. **B.** Call the police and report the incident
5. **D.** It depends on the state you live in
6. **D.** All of the above
7. **A.** Cover the damages to the other driver's vehicle
8. **A.** File a claim with your insurance company
9. **C.** $50,000
10. **C.** To protect you financially in the event of an accident
11. **A.** A valid driver's license is not typically required to register a vehicle in the state in which it is being driven.
12. **A.** Liability insurance
13. **D.** GAP insurance
14. **B.** You will have to pay the remaining damages out of pocket
15. **A.** Your liability insurance

Vehicle registration and insurance exam 5

1. **If you are involved in an accident and you do not have insurance, what can happen?**

A. ☐ You will not be held financially responsible for any damages

B. ☐ You will be required to pay for all damages out of pocket

C. ☐ Your state's uninsured motorist fund will cover the damages

D. ☐ The other party's insurance company will cover the damages

2. **If you are found to be driving without insurance and are involved in an accident, what penalty could you face?**

A. ☐ A fine

B. ☐ A license suspension

C. ☐ A jail sentence

D. ☐ All of the above

3. **In which of the following situations is it NOT required to register a vehicle in the state in which it is being driven?**

A. ☐ The vehicle is owned by a resident of the state

B. ☐ The vehicle is being driven for commercial purposes

C. ☐ The vehicle is being driven for personal use

D. ☐ The vehicle is being driven for a short period of time as a tourist

4. **Which of the following is NOT typically required to obtain insurance for a vehicle?**

A. ☐ A valid driver's license

B. ☐ The vehicle's make and model

C. ☐ The vehicle's VIN number

D. ☐ Payment of any applicable premiums

5. **What is the minimum liability insurance required for a private passenger vehicle in most states?**

A. ☐ $10,000

B. ☐ $25,000

C. ☐ $50,000

D. ☐ $100,000

6. **Which of the following is NOT typically a requirement for maintaining auto insurance coverage?**

A. ☐ Payment of premiums on time

B. ☐ Reporting any accidents or tickets to the insurance company

C. ☐ Reporting any changes in the policyholder's personal or vehicle information

D. ☐ Upgrading the policy to include additional coverage as needed

7. **What is the process for transferring ownership of a vehicle to a new owner?**

A. ☐ The new owner must bring the vehicle to the DMV and fill out a transfer of ownership form

B. ☐ The previous owner must fill out a transfer of ownership form and submit it to the DMV

C. ☐ Both the previous owner and the new owner must fill out a transfer of ownership form and submit it to the DMV

D. ☐ The previous owner must fill out a transfer of ownership form and give it to the new owner, who must then submit it to the DMV

8. **Which of the following is NOT typically covered by a standard auto insurance policy?**

A. ☐ Liability for damages caused by the policyholder to other parties

B. ☐ Damage to the policyholder's own vehicle

C. ☐ Medical expenses for the policyholder and passengers

D. ☐ Property damage caused by natural disasters

9. When is it typically required to register a vehicle in the state in which it is being driven?

A. ☐ When the vehicle is owned by a resident of the state

B. ☐ When the vehicle is being driven for commercial purposes

C. ☐ When the vehicle is being driven for personal use

D. ☐ All of the above

10. What is the purpose of the minimum coverage requirement for auto insurance?

A. ☐ To ensure that policyholders are able to cover the full cost of an accident

B. ☐ To ensure that policyholders have access to additional coverage as needed

C. ☐ To provide a basic level of protection for policyholders and other parties involved in an accident

D. ☐ To ensure that policyholders are able to afford the full cost of an accident

11. Which of the following is NOT typically a factor in determining the cost of auto insurance?

A. ☐ The make and model of the vehicle

B. ☐ The age and driving history of the policyholder

C. ☐ The location in which the vehicle is driven

D. ☐ The policyholder's credit score

12. What happens if a vehicle owner allows their auto insurance coverage to lapse?

A. ☐ The vehicle owner must pay a fine

B. ☐ The vehicle owner must reapply for insurance coverage

C. ☐ The vehicle owner's driver's license may be suspended

D. ☐ All of the above

13. In which of the following situations is it NOT required to have insurance for a vehicle?

A. ☐ The vehicle is being driven for commercial purposes

B. ☐ The vehicle is being driven for personal use

C. ☐ The vehicle is being driven on a public road

D. ☐ The vehicle is being driven on private property

14. Which of the following is NOT typically required to register a vehicle in the state in which it is being driven?

A. ☐ A valid driver's license

B. ☐ Proof of ownership of the vehicle

C. ☐ Proof of insurance for the vehicle

D. ☐ Payment of any applicable fees

15. In which of the following situations would a policyholder's auto insurance coverage typically NOT be extended to a borrowed vehicle?

A. ☐ The policyholder has permission from the owner of the borrowed vehicle to use it

B. ☐ The policyholder is using the borrowed vehicle for personal use

C. ☐ The policyholder is using the borrowed vehicle for commercial purposes

D. ☐ The policyholder is using the borrowed vehicle for a short period of time as a tourist

Correct answers for vehicle registration and insurance exam 5

1. **B.** You will be required to pay for all damages out of pocket

2. **D.** All of the above

3. **D.** It is not typically required to register a vehicle in the state in which it is being driven if the vehicle is being driven for a short period of time as a tourist.

4. **D.** Payment of any applicable premiums is not typically required to obtain insurance for a vehicle.

5. **C.** $50,000

6. **D.** Upgrading the policy to include additional coverage as needed is not typically a requirement for maintaining auto insurance coverage.

7. **C.** Both the previous owner and the new owner must fill out a transfer of ownership form and submit it to the DMV

8. **D.** Property damage caused by natural disasters is not typically covered by a standard auto insurance policy.

9. **D.** All of the above (when the vehicle is owned by a resident of the state, when the vehicle is being driven for commercial purposes, and when the vehicle is being driven for personal use) are typically required to register a vehicle in the state in which it is being driven.

10. **C.** The minimum coverage requirement for auto insurance is to provide a basic level of protection for policyholders and other parties involved in an accident.

11. **D.** The policyholder's credit score is not typically a factor in determining the cost of auto insurance.

12. **D.** All of the above (the vehicle owner must pay a fine, the vehicle owner must reapply for insurance coverage, and the vehicle owner's driver's license may be suspended) happen if a vehicle owner allows their auto insurance coverage to lapse.

13. **D.** It is not typically required to have insurance for a vehicle that is being driven on private property.

14. **A.** A valid driver's license is not typically required to register a vehicle in the state in which it is being driven.

15. **C.** The policyholder's auto insurance coverage typically would NOT be extended to a borrowed vehicle that is being used for commercial purposes.

Emergencies

Driving is an essential part of everyday life for many people in California. It allows us to get to work, run errands, and visit friends and family. However, driving also carries with it a significant amount of responsibility. It is important for all drivers to be aware of and follow the rules of the road in order to ensure the safety of themselves and others. One important way to demonstrate your knowledge of these rules is by passing the California Practice Driving Test.

The California Practice Driving Test is designed to evaluate your knowledge of the rules of the road and your ability to safely operate a motor vehicle. It consists of a written portion and a behind-the-wheel portion. The written portion covers topics such as traffic laws, road signs, and safe driving practices. The behind-the-wheel portion involves actually driving a vehicle with the supervision of a licensed driving instructor.

While the California Practice Driving Test is a routine part of getting a driver's license, it can also be a source of stress for some individuals. It is natural to feel nervous about taking a test, especially one that has the potential to affect your ability to drive. However, with proper preparation and a clear understanding of what to expect, it is possible to successfully pass the California Practice Driving Test on the first try.

In this chapter, we will provide a detailed overview of the California Practice Driving Test, including what to expect on both the written and behind-the-wheel portions. We will also discuss strategies for preparing for the test and offer tips for ensuring a successful outcome. In addition, we will address common mistakes that people make during the test and provide suggestions for avoiding them.

Overall, our goal is to provide you with the knowledge and confidence you need to successfully pass the California Practice Driving Test on your first attempt. With proper preparation and a clear understanding of what to expect, you can confidently take the test and move one step closer to obtaining your driver's license.

For training purposes, you can mark the ☐ symbol next to what you think is the correct answer: Once you have chosen the correct answer, use a pencil or pen to mark the ☐ symbol next to that answer.

So, let's get started!

Emergencies exam

1. **What should you do if your vehicle begins to skid on a slippery road surface?**

A. ☐ Brake hard

B. ☐ Steer in the direction of the skid

C. ☐ Steer in the opposite direction of the skid

D. ☐ Accelerate

2. **You are driving on a highway and the vehicle in front of you is stopped in the left lane. You should:**

A. ☐ Slow down and move to the right lane

B. ☐ Honk your horn and pass on the right

C. ☐ Slow down and pass on the left

D. ☐ Honk your horn and pass on the left

3. **You are driving and the vehicle in front of you suddenly stops. You should:**

A. ☐ Swerve to the right to avoid the vehicle

B. ☐ Brake hard and come to a complete stop

C. ☐ Steer around the vehicle

D. ☐ Honk your horn and keep driving

4. **You are driving on a highway and see a pedestrian on the side of the road waving their arms. You should:**

A. ☐ Slow down and be prepared to stop

B. ☐ Honk your horn and keep driving

C. ☐ Speed up and pass quickly

D. ☐ Swerve to the left to avoid the pedestrian

5. You are driving and your vehicle runs out of fuel. You should:

A. ☐ Pull over to the side of the road and call for help

B. ☐ Continue driving and hope to find a gas station soon

C. ☐ Get out of the vehicle and push it to the nearest gas station

D. ☐ Flag down a passing vehicle and ask for a ride to the nearest gas station

6. You are driving and your vehicle suddenly loses power. You should:

A. ☐ Pull over to the side of the road and call for help

B. ☐ Try to restart the vehicle

C. ☐ Continue driving and hope the problem goes away

D. ☐ Flag down a passing vehicle and ask for a ride

7. You are driving and your vehicle catches on fire. You should:

A. ☐ Pull over to the side of the road and call for help

B. ☐ Try to put out the fire yourself

C. ☐ Continue driving and hope the fire goes out on its own

D. ☐ Flag down a passing vehicle and ask for help

8. You are driving and your vehicle starts to smoke. You should:

A. ☐ Pull over to the side of the road and call for help

B. ☐ Try to find the source of the smoke and fix the problem

C. ☐ Continue driving and hope the smoke goes away

D. ☐ Flag down a passing vehicle and ask for a ride

9. You are driving and your vehicle gets a flat tire. You should:

A. ☐ Pull over to the side of the road and call for help

B. ☐ Try to change the tire yourself

C. ☐ Continue driving and hope the tire holds out

D. ☐ Flag down a passing vehicle and ask for a ride

10. You are driving and your vehicle experiences a mechanical failure. You should:

A. ☐ Pull over to the side of the road and call for help

B. ☐ Try to fix the problem yourself

C. ☐ Continue driving and hope the problem goes away

D. ☐ Flag down a passing vehicle and ask for a ride

11. You are driving and your vehicle's engine starts making a strange noise. What should you do?

A. ☐ Ignore the noise and continue driving

B. ☐ Pull over to the side of the road and call for help

C. ☐ Try to diagnose the problem yourself

D. ☐ Flag down a passing vehicle and ask for a ride

12. You are driving and your vehicle's brakes fail. What should you do?

A. ☐ Panic and slam on the brakes

B. ☐ Downshift and use the engine to slow down

C. ☐ Use the emergency brake

D. ☐ Honk your horn and continue driving

13. You are driving and your vehicle's steering becomes difficult to control. What should you do?

A. ☐ Pull over to the side of the road and call for help

B. ☐ Try to diagnose the problem yourself

C. ☐ Continue driving and hope the problem goes away

D. ☐ Flag down a passing vehicle and ask for a ride

14. You are driving and your vehicle's transmission fails. What should you do?

A. ☐ Pull over to the side of the road and call for help

B. ☐ Try to fix the problem yourself

C. ☐ Continue driving and hope the problem goes away

D. ☐ Flag down a passing vehicle and ask for a ride

15. You are driving and your vehicle's battery dies. What should you do?

A. ☐ Pull over to the side of the road and call for help

B. ☐ Try to jump start the vehicle

C. ☐ Continue driving and hope the battery recharges itself

D. ☐ Flag down a passing vehicle and ask for a ride

Correct answers for emergencies exam

1. **C.** Steer in the opposite direction of the skid

2. **A.** Slow down and move to the right lane

3. **B.** Brake hard and come to a complete stop

4. **A.** Slow down and be prepared to stop

5. **A.** Pull over to the side of the road and call for help

6. **A.** Pull over to the side of the road and call for help

7. **A.** Pull over to the side of the road and call for help

8. **A.** Pull over to the side of the road and call for help

9. **B.** Try to change the tire yourself

10. **A.** Pull over to the side of the road and call for help

11. **B.** Pull over to the side of the road and call for help

12. **C.** Use the emergency brake

13. **A.** Pull over to the side of the road and call for help

14. **A.** Pull over to the side of the road and call for help

15. **B.** Try to jump start the vehicle

Emergencies exam 2

1. **What should you do if your car starts to hydroplane while driving in heavy rain?**

   A. ☐ Slow down and carefully steer in the direction you want the car to go.

   B. ☐ Brake hard and steer in the direction you want the car to go.

   C. ☐ Accelerate and steer in the direction you want the car to go.

   D. ☐ Turn off the engine and coast to a stop.

2. **Your car's engine suddenly loses power while driving on the highway. What should you do?**

   A. ☐ Pull over to the side of the road and turn off the engine.

   B. ☐ Try to restart the engine while driving.

   C. ☐ Shift into neutral and coast to a stop.

   D. ☐ Use your hazard lights and continue driving at a reduced speed.

3. **You are driving and see a pedestrian about to step into the road in front of you. What should you do?**

   A. ☐ Honk your horn to warn the pedestrian.

   B. ☐ Swerve around the pedestrian.

   C. ☐ Apply the brakes and come to a stop.

   D. ☐ Accelerate to get through the intersection quickly.

4. **You are driving on a mountain road and your brakes suddenly fail. What should you do?**

   A. ☐ Shift into a lower gear to use engine braking.

   B. ☐ Use the emergency brake to try to slow down.

   C. ☐ Pump the brake pedal rapidly to try to build up brake fluid pressure.

   D. ☐ Steer off the road and try to stop the car by running into a ditch or other soft surface.

5. **You are driving on a highway and your steering suddenly becomes very difficult to turn. What could be the cause of this problem?**

A. ☐ A blown tire

B. ☐ A broken steering pump

C. ☐ A loose steering wheel

D. ☐ A faulty steering column

6. **Your car's check engine light comes on while driving. What should you do?**

A. ☐ Ignore the light and continue driving.

B. ☐ Pull over and turn off the engine.

C. ☐ Drive to the nearest repair shop.

D. ☐ Check the owner's manual for troubleshooting tips.

7. **You are driving on a highway and your car starts to shake violently. What could be the cause of this problem?**

A. ☐ A blown tire

B. ☐ A faulty transmission

C. ☐ A misaligned suspension

D. ☐ A faulty exhaust system

8. **You are driving and notice a strong burning smell coming from your car. What should you do?**

A. ☐ Turn off the air conditioning and roll down the windows.

B. ☐ Turn off the engine and pull over to the side of the road.

C. ☐ Open the hood to see if you can identify the source of the smell.

D. ☐ Continue driving and try to get to a repair shop as quickly as possible.

9. Your car's battery dies while driving. What should you do?

A. ☐ Try to jump start the car using jumper cables.

B. ☐ Call a tow truck to take you to a repair shop.

C. ☐ Push the car to the side of the road and call for help.

D. ☐ Try to flag down a passing motorist for assistance.

10. You are driving and see a traffic jam ahead. What should you do?

A. ☐ Change lanes to try to get around the traffic.

B. ☐ Slow down and merge into the traffic when there is an opening.

C. ☐ Speed up and try to get through the traffic before it becomes too congested.

D. ☐ Use the shoulder to bypass the traffic.

11. Your car's engine starts to overheat while driving. What should you do?

A. ☐ Continue driving and try to get to a repair shop as quickly as possible.

B. ☐ Turn off the air conditioning and roll down the windows.

C. ☐ Turn off the engine and wait for the car to cool down.

D. ☐ Open the hood to see if you can identify the source of the problem.

12. You are driving and your car's oil pressure warning light comes on. What should you do?

A. ☐ Ignore the light and continue driving.

B. ☐ Pull over to the side of the road and turn off the engine.

C. ☐ Check the oil level and add more oil if needed.

D. ☐ Drive to the nearest repair shop.

13. You are driving and your car's fuel gauge indicates that you are running low on gas. What should you do?

A. ☐ Continue driving until the car runs out of gas.

B. ☐ Pull over to the side of the road and call for help.

C. ☐ Try to coast to the nearest gas station.

D. ☐ Fill up the gas tank as soon as possible.

14. You are driving and your car's transmission fails. What should you do?

A. ☐ Shift into a lower gear and continue driving.

B. ☐ Shift into neutral and coast to a stop.

C. ☐ Turn off the engine and call for a tow truck.

D. ☐ Try to restart the engine and continue driving.

15. You are driving and your car's brakes fail. What should you do?

A. ☐ Try to use the emergency brake to stop the car.

B. ☐ Shift into a lower gear and use engine braking to slow down.

C. ☐ Turn off the engine and coast to a stop.

D. ☐ Steer off the road and try to stop the car by running into a ditch or other soft surface.

Correct answers for emergencies exam 2

1. **A.** Slow down and carefully steer in the direction you want the car to go. Hydroplaning occurs when the tires lose contact with the road surface due to a film of water between the tire and the road. Sudden movements, such as braking hard or steering sharply, can cause the car to lose control. The correct course of action is to reduce your speed and gently steer in the direction you want the car to go to regain traction.

2. **A.** Pull over to the side of the road and turn off the engine. If the engine suddenly loses power while driving, it is important to safely bring the car to a stop as soon as possible. Pulling over to the side of the road and turning off the engine can prevent further damage to the car and allow you to assess the situation.

3. **C.** Apply the brakes and come to a stop. If a pedestrian is about to step into the road in front of you, it is important to stop the car to prevent a collision. Applying the brakes and coming to a stop is the safest course of action in this situation.

4. **A.** Shift into a lower gear to use engine braking. If the brakes fail while driving on a mountain road, it is important to try to slow down the car as much as possible to avoid a collision. Shifting into a lower gear can help to use the engine to brake and slow the car down.

5. **A.** A blown tire. If the steering becomes difficult to turn while driving, it could be caused by a blown tire. A flat or damaged tire can cause the car to pull to one side and make steering difficult. Other potential causes of steering problems include a broken steering pump, a loose steering wheel, or a faulty steering column.

6. **D.** Check the owner's manual for troubleshooting tips. If the check engine light comes on while driving, it is important to address the issue as soon as possible to prevent further damage to the car. Checking the owner's manual can provide guidance on troubleshooting and identifying the source of the problem.

7. **A.** A blown tire. If the car starts shaking violently while driving, it could be caused by a blown tire. A flat or damaged tire can cause the car to vibrate and shake. Other potential causes of shaking include a faulty transmission, a misaligned suspension, or a faulty exhaust system.

8. **B.** Turn off the engine and pull over to the side of the road. If you notice a strong burning smell coming from your car while driving, it is important to stop the car as soon as possible to prevent a fire. Turning off the engine and pulling over to the side of the road can help to prevent further damage to the car and allow you to assess the situation.

9. **A.** Try to jump start the car using jumper cables. If the car's battery dies while driving, you can try to jump start the car using jumper cables to get the engine running again. If the battery is completely dead or the jumper cables are not working, you may need to call a tow truck or flag down a passing motorist for assistance.

10. **B.** Slow down and merge into the traffic when there is an opening. If you see a traffic jam ahead while driving, it is important to slow down and be prepared to stop. Merging into the traffic when there is an opening can help to prevent a collision. Other options, such as changing lanes or using the shoulder to bypass the traffic, can be dangerous and should be avoided.

11. **C.** Turn off the engine and wait for the car to cool down. If the car's engine starts to overheat while driving, it is important to stop the car and allow the engine to cool down. Continuing to drive can cause further damage to the engine and potentially result in a breakdown. Turning off the engine and waiting for the car to cool down can help to prevent further problems.

12. **B.** Pull over to the side of the road and turn off the engine. If the oil pressure warning light comes on while driving, it is important to stop the car as soon as possible to prevent further damage. Pulling over to the side of the road and turning off the engine can help to prevent further problems and allow you to assess the situation.

13. **D.** Fill up the gas tank as soon as possible. If the fuel gauge indicates that you are running low on gas, it is important to fill up the gas tank as soon as possible to prevent the car from running out of gas. Running out of gas can cause the car to break down and potentially result in a dangerous situation.

14. **C.** Turn off the engine and call for a tow truck. If the car's transmission fails while driving, it is important to stop the car as soon as possible to prevent further damage. Turning off the engine and calling for a tow truck can help to get the car safely off the road and to a repair shop.

15. **D.** Steer off the road and try to stop the car by running into a ditch or other soft surface. If the brakes fail while driving, it is important to try to stop the car as safely as possible to prevent a collision. Steering off the road and trying to stop the car by running into a ditch or other soft surface can help to slow the car down and prevent further problems. Other options, such as trying to use the emergency brake or shifting into a lower gear, may not be effective in stopping the car.

Emergencies exam 3

1. **What should you do if your car starts to hydroplane?**

   A. ☐ Slow down gradually

   B. ☐ Apply the brakes firmly

   C. ☐ Steer in the direction you want the front of the car to go

   D. ☐ All of the above

2. **What should you do if your car engine catches fire while driving?**

   A. ☐ Pull over to the side of the road as soon as possible

   B. ☐ Put the fire out using a fire extinguisher

   C. ☐ Continue driving until you reach a gas station

   D. ☐ Open the hood to let the fire burn out

3. **What should you do if you get a flat tire while driving?**

   A. ☐ Continue driving until you reach a repair shop

   B. ☐ Use a spare tire if you have one

   C. ☐ Try to repair the flat tire using a tire patch kit

   D. ☐ All of the above

4. **What should you do if your car's accelerator gets stuck while driving?**

   A. ☐ Shift the car into neutral and coast to a stop

   B. ☐ Turn the ignition off

   C. ☐ Use the emergency brake to stop the car

   D. ☐ Apply the brakes firmly

5. What should you do if your car's steering becomes unresponsive while driving?

A. ☐ Turn the steering wheel in the opposite direction of the way the car is going

B. ☐ Shift the car into neutral and coast to a stop

C. ☐ Apply the brakes firmly

D. ☐ Turn the ignition off

6. What should you do if your car's brakes fail while driving?

A. ☐ Shift the car into neutral and coast to a stop

B. ☐ Use the emergency brake to stop the car

C. ☐ Pump the brakes repeatedly

D. ☐ Turn the ignition off

7. What should you do if your car runs out of gas while driving?

A. ☐ Shift the car into neutral and coast to a stop

B. ☐ Turn the ignition off

C. ☐ Exit the car and push it to the side of the road

D. ☐ Call for help and wait for assistance

8. What should you do if your car's battery dies while driving?

A. ☐ Turn the ignition off and try to start the car again

B. ☐ Shift the car into neutral and coast to a stop

C. ☐ Use jumper cables to try to start the car

D. ☐ All of the above

9. What should you do if your car's tires become bald while driving?

A. ☐ Continue driving as normal

B. ☐ Shift the car into neutral and coast to a stop

C. ☐ Use a spare tire if you have one

D. ☐ Call for help and wait for assistance

10. What should you do if you see smoke or flames coming from the hood of your car while driving?

A. ☐ Continue driving until you reach a repair shop

B. ☐ Shift the car into neutral and coast to a stop

C. ☐ Try to put the fire out using a fire extinguisher

D. ☐ Pull over to the side of the road as soon as possible

11. What should you do if your car's steering wheel becomes stuck while driving?

A. ☐ Shift the car into neutral and coast to a stop

B. ☐ Turn the ignition off

C. ☐ Use the emergency brake to stop the car

D. ☐ Apply the brakes firmly

12. What should you do if your car's transmission fails while driving?

A. ☐ Shift the car into neutral and coast to a stop

B. ☐ Turn the ignition off

C. ☐ Use the emergency brake to stop the car

D. ☐ Apply the brakes firmly

13. What should you do if your car's radiator overheats while driving?

A. ☐ Shift the car into neutral and coast to a stop

B. ☐ Turn the ignition off

C. ☐ Use the emergency brake to stop the car

D. ☐ Turn off the air conditioning and open the windows

14. What should you do if your car's fuel pump fails while driving?

A. ☐ Shift the car into neutral and coast to a stop

B. ☐ Turn the ignition off

C. ☐ Use the emergency brake to stop the car

D. ☐ Apply the brakes firmly

15. What should you do if your car's alternator fails while driving?

A. ☐ Shift the car into neutral and coast to a stop

B. ☐ Turn the ignition off

C. ☐ Use the emergency brake to stop the car

D. ☐ Apply the brakes firmly

Correct answers for emergencies exam 3

1. **C.** If your car starts to hydroplane, steer in the direction you want the front of the car to go.

2. **A.** If your car engine catches fire while driving, pull over to the side of the road as soon as possible.

3. **B.** If you get a flat tire while driving, use a spare tire if you have one.

4. **A.** If your car's accelerator gets stuck while driving, shift the car into neutral and coast to a stop.

5. **A.** If your car's steering becomes unresponsive while driving, turn the steering wheel in the opposite direction of the way the car is going.

6. **B.** If your car's brakes fail while driving, use the emergency brake to stop the car.

7. **D.** If your car runs out of gas while driving, call for help and wait for assistance.

8. **A.** If your car's battery dies while driving, turn the ignition off and try to start the car again.

9. **C.** If your car's tires become bald while driving, use a spare tire if you have one.

10. **D.** If you see smoke or flames coming from the hood of your car while driving, pull over to the side of the road as soon as possible.

11. **A.** If your car's steering wheel becomes stuck while driving, shift the car into neutral and coast to a stop.

12. **A.** If your car's transmission fails while driving, shift the car into neutral and coast to a stop.

13. **D.** If your car's radiator overheats while driving, turn off the air conditioning and open the windows.

14. **A.** If your car's fuel pump fails while driving, shift the car into neutral and coast to a stop.

15. **A.** If your car's alternator fails while driving, shift the car into neutral and coast to a stop.

Emergencies exam 4

1. **When driving in heavy rain, it is important to use which of the following techniques to increase visibility?**

   A. ☐ Turn on your high beams

   B. ☐ Increase your following distance

   C. ☐ Use your wipers and defroster

   D. ☐ Flash your lights at oncoming cars

2. **If your vehicle starts to skid on a slippery road, which of the following actions should you take?**

   A. ☐ Turn the steering wheel in the direction of the skid

   B. ☐ Brake hard to stop the skid

   C. ☐ Turn the steering wheel in the opposite direction of the skid

   D. ☐ Accelerate to try and regain control

3. **While driving, your car suddenly loses power. What should you do?**

   A. ☐ Pull over to the side of the road and call for help

   B. ☐ Keep driving and try to make it to your destination

   C. ☐ Turn on your hazard lights and drive slowly

   D. ☐ Try to restart the engine

4. **You are driving on a highway when you see a tire on the road ahead. What should you do?**

   A. ☐ Brake hard and try to avoid the tire

   B. ☐ Swerve to the left or right to avoid the tire

   C. ☐ Keep driving straight and hope that the tire misses your car

   D. ☐ Signal and change lanes before slowly driving over the tire

5. You are driving on a highway when a car in the lane next to you starts to lose control. What should you do?

A. ☐ Speed up to get out of the way

B. ☐ Slow down and give the other car plenty of room

C. ☐ Honk your horn to try to alert the other driver

D. ☐ Try to steer the other car back into control

6. When driving through a construction zone, you should:

A. ☐ Slow down and be prepared to stop

B. ☐ Speed up to get through the zone as quickly as possible

C. ☐ Honk your horn to alert the workers

D. ☐ Ignore any signs or signals and drive as you normally would

7. You are driving in heavy rain and your windshield wipers are not working properly. What should you do?

A. ☐ Turn on your hazard lights and pull over to the side of the road

B. ☐ Try to clean the wipers with a cloth

C. ☐ Turn on your headlights to improve visibility

D. ☐ Open your window to try to clear the rain from the windshield

8. You are driving on a highway when you hear a loud noise coming from your car. What should you do?

A. ☐ Ignore the noise and keep driving

B. ☐ Pull over to the side of the road and call for help

C. ☐ Turn up the volume on the radio to drown out the noise

D. ☐ Accelerate to try to outrun the noise

9. If your vehicle becomes disabled on the side of the road, you should:

A. ☐ Leave the vehicle and try to flag down help

B. ☐ Stay in the vehicle and wait for help

C. ☐ Try to fix the problem yourself

D. ☐ Abandon the vehicle and try to walk to safety

10. You are driving on a highway and your steering becomes difficult to control. What should you do?

A. ☐ Pull over to the side of the road and call for help

B. ☐ Try to adjust the steering wheel to regain control

C. ☐ Continue driving and try to reach your destination

D. ☐ Turn on your hazard lights and drive slowly

11. You are driving on a highway and see a vehicle with its hazard lights on parked on the shoulder. You should:

A. ☐ Slow down and pass with caution

B. ☐ Speed up and pass as quickly as possible

C. ☐ Change lanes if it is safe to do so

D. ☐ Stop and offer assistance if you are able

12. If you are driving and see a school bus with its red lights flashing and stop sign extended, you should:

A. ☐ Slow down and be prepared to stop

B. ☐ Speed up to pass the bus quickly

C. ☐ Honk your horn to alert the bus driver

D. ☐ Ignore the bus and continue driving

13. If your vehicle's engine catches fire, you should:

A. ☐ Try to extinguish the fire using a fire extinguisher or other means

B. ☐ Abandon the vehicle and call for help

C. ☐ Try to drive to a safe location

D. ☐ Stay inside the vehicle and wait for help

14. If you are involved in a collision, you should:

A. ☐ Leave the scene as quickly as possible

B. ☐ Exchange information with the other driver and call the police

C. ☐ Try to move the vehicles out of the way to clear the road

D. ☐ Ignore the collision and continue driving

15. If you see a pedestrian using a white cane or guide dog, you should:

A. ☐ Honk your horn to get their attention

B. ☐ Proceed with caution and be prepared to stop

C. ☐ Speed up to pass them quickly

D. ☐ Ignore them and drive as you normally would

Correct answers for emergencies exam 4

1. **C.** Use your wipers and defroster
2. **C.** Turn the steering wheel in the opposite direction of the skid
3. **A.** Slow down and pass with caution
4. **D.** - Signal and change lanes before slowly driving over the tire
5. **A.** Try to extinguish the fire using a fire extinguisher or other means
6. **A.** Slow down and be prepared to stop
7. **A.** - Turn on your hazard lights and pull over to the side of the road
8. **B.** Proceed with caution and be prepared to stop
9. **B.** Stay in the vehicle and wait for help
10. **A.** Slow down and be prepared to stop
11. **A.** Slow down and pass with caution
12. **A.** Slow down and be prepared to stop
13. **A.** Try to extinguish the fire using a fire extinguisher or other means
14. **B.** Exchange information with the other driver and call the police
15. **B.** Proceed with caution and be prepared to stop

Emergencies exam 5

1. **If you are driving and your vehicle starts to hydroplane, which of the following actions should you take?**

   A. ☐ Apply the brakes

   B. ☐ Steer in the direction of the skid

   C. ☐ Steer in the opposite direction of the skid

   D. ☐ Accelerate to try and regain control

2. **You are driving on a highway when you see a car on the side of the road with its hazard lights on. What should you do?**

   A. ☐ Keep driving and ignore the other car

   B. ☐ Slow down and be prepared to stop if necessary

   C. ☐ Change lanes to give the other car plenty of room

   D. ☐ Flash your headlights to try to get the other driver's attention

3. **If you are driving and your vehicle's tires become punctured, you should:**

   A. ☐ Attempt to fix the tire yourself

   B. ☐ Pull over and change the tire

   C. ☐ Continue driving on the flat tire

   D. ☐ Abandon the vehicle and seek help

4. **If you are driving and your vehicle's engine overheats, you should:**

   A. ☐ Turn off the air conditioning and open the windows

   B. ☐ Turn off the engine and call for help

   C. ☐ Continue driving and hope the problem goes away

   D. ☐ Try to find a safe place to stop and let the engine cool down

5. **If you are driving on a highway and see a vehicle with its hazard lights on parked on the shoulder, you should:**

A. ☐ Slow down and pass with caution

B. ☐ Speed up and pass as quickly as possible

C. ☐ Change lanes if it is safe to do so

D. ☐ Stop and offer assistance if you are able

6. **If you are driving and your vehicle's brakes fail, you should:**

A. ☐ Shift into a lower gear and use engine braking

B. ☐ Use the emergency brake

C. ☐ Try to steer off the road and onto the shoulder

D. ☐ Abandon the vehicle and seek help

7. **If you are driving and you see a school bus with its red lights flashing and stop sign extended, you should:**

A. ☐ Slow down and be prepared to stop

B. ☐ Speed up to pass the bus quickly

C. ☐ Honk your horn to alert the bus driver

D. ☐ Ignore the bus and continue driving

8. **If you are driving and your vehicle becomes disabled on the side of the road, you should:**

A. ☐ Leave the vehicle and try to flag down help

B. ☐ Stay in the vehicle and wait for help

C. ☐ Try to fix the problem yourself

D. ☐ Abandon the vehicle and try to walk to safety

9. **If you are driving and your vehicle starts to skid on a slippery road, which of the following actions should you take?**

A. ☐ Turn the steering wheel in the direction of the skid

B. ☐ Brake hard to stop the skid

C. ☐ Turn the steering wheel in the opposite direction of the skid

D. ☐ Accelerate to try and regain control

10. **If you are driving and your vehicle's engine catches fire, you should:**

A. ☐ Try to extinguish the fire using a fire extinguisher or other means

B. ☐ Abandon the vehicle and call for help

C. ☐ Try to drive to a safe location

D. ☐ Stay inside the vehicle and wait for help

11. **What is the first thing you should do if you experience a tire blowout while driving?**

A. ☐ Slow down gradually and pull to the side of the road

B. ☐ Accelerate to try and make it to the next exit

C. ☐ Slam on the brakes and come to a stop as quickly as possible

D. ☐ Try to steer the vehicle in the direction of the blowout

12. **If your car begins to skid on a slippery road, which of the following actions should you NOT take?**

A. ☐ Remove your foot from the accelerator and allow the vehicle to slow down on its own

B. ☐ Look and steer in the direction you want the car to go

C. ☐ Turn the steering wheel sharply in the opposite direction of the skid

D. ☐ Gently apply the brakes to regain control of the vehicle

13. You are driving on a highway and your engine suddenly loses power. What should you do?

A. ☐ Try to restart the engine

B. ☐ Shift into neutral and coast to the side of the road

C. ☐ Hold the steering wheel firmly and try to maintain control of the vehicle

D. ☐ Immediately apply the brakes and come to a stop

14. You are driving in heavy rain and your visibility is severely reduced. What should you do?

A. ☐ Turn on your high beams to help see better

B. ☐ Increase your speed to get through the rain more quickly

C. ☐ Use your hazard lights to warn other drivers of your reduced visibility

D. ☐ Slow down and increase the distance between your vehicle and the one in front of you

15. You are driving on a highway and see a car on the shoulder with its hazard lights on. What should you do?

A. ☐ Speed up and pass the stopped vehicle as quickly as possible

B. ☐ Merge into the left lane to give the stopped vehicle plenty of room

C. ☐ Slow down and be prepared to stop if necessary

D. ☐ Honk your horn to alert the driver of the stopped vehicle

Correct answers for emergencies exam 5

1. **C.** Steer in the opposite direction of the skid

2. **B.** Slow down and be prepared to stop if necessary

3. **B.** Pull over and change the tire

4. **D.** Try to find a safe place to stop and let the engine cool down

5. **A.** Slow down and pass with caution

6. **A.** Shift into a lower gear and use engine braking

7. **A.** Slow down and be prepared to stop

8. **B.** Stay in the vehicle and wait for help

9. **C.** Turn the steering wheel in the opposite direction of the skid

10. **A.** Try to extinguish the fire using a fire extinguisher or other means

11. **A.** Slow down gradually and pull to the side of the road

12. **C.** Turn the steering wheel sharply in the opposite direction of the skid

13. **B.** Shift into neutral and coast to the side of the road

14. **D.** Slow down and increase the distance between your vehicle and the one in front of you

15. **B.** Merge into the left lane to give the stopped vehicle plenty of room

Vehicle size and weight limits

Vehicle size and weight limits are an important aspect of driving safely on the roads in California. Ensuring that a vehicle is within the legal size and weight limits can help prevent accidents and damage to infrastructure. It is essential for all drivers to understand these limits and to follow them at all times.

In this chapter, we will explore the various size and weight limits that apply to vehicles in California. We will also discuss the importance of adhering to these limits, as well as the consequences of violating them. Additionally, we will provide information on the practice driving tests that are required in California, and how they can help drivers learn and understand the rules and regulations related to vehicle size and weight limits.

California has strict size and weight limits in place for vehicles operating on its roads. These limits are designed to ensure the safety of all road users, as well as to protect the integrity of the road infrastructure. It is important for drivers to be aware of these limits and to ensure that their vehicles are in compliance.

The size limits in California apply to the overall dimensions of a vehicle, including its length, width, and height. There are also specific size limits for certain types of vehicles, such as buses and trailers. These limits help to ensure that vehicles can safely navigate the roads, and that they do not pose a risk to other road users or to infrastructure.

In addition to size limits, there are also weight limits for vehicles operating in California. These limits are designed to ensure that vehicles do not exceed the maximum allowable weight for the roads they are traveling on. Exceeding these limits can cause damage to the roads and can increase the risk of accidents. It is important for drivers to understand and adhere to these limits to ensure the safety of all road users.

In California, all drivers are required to pass a practice driving test in order to obtain a driver's license. These tests are designed to ensure that drivers have a good understanding of the rules and regulations related to vehicle size and weight limits, as well as other important aspects of safe driving. The practice driving test consists of both a written exam and a practical driving test, which are designed to assess the knowledge and skills of the driver.

By understanding and adhering to the size and weight limits for vehicles in California, drivers can help to ensure the safety of themselves and others on the road. The practice driving tests required in California can also help drivers learn and understand these important regulations, and can help to prepare them for safe driving on the roads of California.

For training purposes, you can mark the ☐ symbol next to what you think is the correct answer: Once you have chosen the correct answer, use a pencil or pen to mark the ☐ symbol next to that answer.

Vehicle size and weight limits exam

1. **What is the maximum width allowed for a vehicle in California?**

    A. ☐ 8 feet 6 inches

    B. ☐ 9 feet 6 inches

    C. ☐ 10 feet 6 inches

    D. ☐ 11 feet 6 inches

2. **What is the maximum length allowed for a single vehicle in California?**

    A. ☐ 45 feet

    B. ☐ 50 feet

    C. ☐ 55 feet

    D. ☐ 60 feet

3. **What is the maximum length allowed for a combination of vehicles, including a towing vehicle and trailer?**

    A. ☐ 65 feet

    B. ☐ 70 feet

    C. ☐ 75 feet

    D. ☐ 80 feet

4. **What is the maximum weight allowed for a single vehicle in California?**

    A. ☐ 8,000 pounds

    B. ☐ 10,000 pounds

    C. ☐ 12,000 pounds

    D. ☐ 14,000 pounds

5. What is the maximum weight allowed for a combination of vehicles, including a towing vehicle and trailer?

A. ☐ 16,000 pounds

B. ☐ 18,000 pounds

C. ☐ 20,000 pounds

D. ☐ 22,000 pounds

6. Are there any exceptions to the size and weight limits for vehicles in California?

A. ☐ No, there are no exceptions.

B. ☐ Yes, exceptions may be made for certain types of vehicles, such as farm vehicles or emergency vehicles.

C. ☐ Yes, exceptions may be made for vehicles transporting hazardous materials.

D. ☐ Both B and C are correct.

7. Is it legal to exceed the size and weight limits for a vehicle in California if it is being used for personal use?

A. ☐ Yes, as long as the vehicle is being used for personal use, it is legal to exceed the size and weight limits.

B. ☐ No, it is never legal to exceed the size and weight limits for a vehicle in California.

C. ☐ Yes, as long as the vehicle is being used for personal use and is not being driven on a public road, it is legal to exceed the size and weight limits.

D. ☐ Yes, as long as the vehicle is being used for personal use and is not being driven on a public road during peak hours, it is legal to exceed the size and weight limits.

8. **If a driver is found to be operating a vehicle that exceeds the size and weight limits in California, what are the potential consequences?**

   A. ☐ The driver may be fined and have points added to their license.
   B. ☐ The driver may have their license suspended or revoked.
   C. ☐ The vehicle may be impounded.
   D. ☐ All of the above are potential consequences.

9. **What is the maximum allowable gross weight for a single vehicle in the United States?**

   A. ☐ 26,000 pounds
   B. ☐ 80,000 pounds
   C. ☐ 100,000 pounds
   D. ☐ No maximum weight limit

10. **What is the maximum allowable gross weight for a combination of vehicles in the United States?**

    A. ☐ 26,000 pounds
    B. ☐ 80,000 pounds
    C. ☐ 100,000 pounds
    D. ☐ No maximum weight limit

11. **What is the maximum height allowed for a vehicle in California?**

    A. ☐ 12 feet
    B. ☐ 13 feet
    C. ☐ 14 feet
    D. ☐ 15 feet

12. What is the maximum length allowed for a trailer in California?

A. ☐ 35 feet

B. ☐ 40 feet

C. ☐ 45 feet

D. ☐ 50 feet

13. Are there any exceptions to the weight limits for vehicles in California based on the type of cargo being transported?

A. ☐ No, weight limits do not vary based on the type of cargo.

B. ☐ Yes, weight limits may be increased for certain types of cargo, such as agricultural products.

C. ☐ Yes, weight limits may be decreased for certain types of cargo, such as hazardous materials.

D. ☐ Both B and C are correct.

14. What is the maximum weight allowed for a single vehicle traveling on a two-lane road in California?

A. ☐ 12,000 pounds

B. ☐ 14,000 pounds

C. ☐ 16,000 pounds

D. ☐ 18,000 pounds

15. Can a driver exceed the size and weight limits for a vehicle in California if they have a special permit from the state?

A. ☐ Yes, a special permit allows a driver to exceed the size and weight limits at any time.

B. ☐ No, a special permit does not allow a driver to exceed the size and weight limits at any time.

C. ☐ Yes, a special permit allows a driver to exceed the size and weight limits in certain circumstances, such as for oversize or overweight loads.

D. ☐ Yes, a special permit allows a driver to exceed the size and weight limits on certain roads, such as designated truck routes.

Correct answers for vehicle size and weight limits exam

1. **A.** 8 feet 6 inches
2. **C.** 55 feet
3. **D.** 80 feet
4. **D.** 14,000 pounds
5. **C.** 20,000 pounds
6. **D.** Both B and C are correct.
7. **B.** No, it is never legal to exceed the size and weight limits for a vehicle in California.
8. **D.** All of the above are potential consequences.
9. **B.** The maximum allowable gross weight for a single vehicle in the United States is 80,000 pounds.
10. **C.** The maximum allowable gross weight for a combination of vehicles in the United States is 100,000 pounds.
11. **A.** 12 feet
12. **D.** 50 feet
13. **D.** Both B and C are correct.
14. **B.** 14,000 pounds
15. **C.** Yes, a special permit allows a driver to exceed the size and weight limits in certain circumstances, such as for oversize or overweight loads.

Vehicle size and weight limits exam 2

1. **What is the maximum weight allowed for a single vehicle traveling on a four-lane road in California?**

   A. ☐ 16,000 pounds
   B. ☐ 18,000 pounds
   C. ☐ 20,000 pounds
   D. ☐ 22,000 pounds

2. What is the maximum weight allowed for a single vehicle traveling on an interstate highway in California?

   A. ☐ 24,000 pounds
   B. ☐ 26,000 pounds
   C. ☐ 28,000 pounds
   D. ☐ 30,000 pounds

3. What is the maximum weight allowed for a combination of vehicles, including a towing vehicle and trailer, traveling on a four-lane road in California?

   A. ☐ 34,000 pounds
   B. ☐ 36,000 pounds
   C. ☐ 38,000 pounds
   D. ☐ 40,000 pounds

4. What is the maximum weight allowed for a combination of vehicles, including a towing vehicle and trailer, traveling on an interstate highway in California?

- **A.** ☐ 42,000 pounds
- **B.** ☐ 44,000 pounds
- **C.** ☐ 46,000 pounds
- **D.** ☐ 48,000 pounds

5. What is the maximum length allowed for a combination of vehicles, including a towing vehicle and trailer, when traveling on a four-lane road in California?

- **A.** ☐ 65 feet
- **B.** ☐ 70 feet
- **C.** ☐ 75 feet
- **D.** ☐ 80 feet

6. What is the maximum length allowed for a combination of vehicles, including a towing vehicle and trailer, when traveling on an interstate highway in California?

- **A.** ☐ 85 feet
- **B.** ☐ 90 feet
- **C.** ☐ 95 feet
- **D.** ☐ 100 feet

7. Is it legal to exceed the size and weight limits for a vehicle in California if it is being used for commercial purposes?

A. ☐ Yes, it is legal to exceed the size and weight limits for a commercial vehicle as long as it is properly registered and has the necessary permits.

B. ☐ No, it is never legal to exceed the size and weight limits for a vehicle in California.

C. ☐ Yes, it is legal to exceed the size and weight limits for a commercial vehicle as long as it is not being driven on a public road.

D. ☐ Yes, it is legal to exceed the size and weight limits for a commercial vehicle as long as it is not being driven on a public road during peak hours.

8. If a driver is found to be operating a vehicle that exceeds the size and weight limits in California, what are the potential consequences for the owner of the vehicle?

A. ☐ The owner of the vehicle may be fined and have points added to their license.

B. ☐ The owner of the vehicle may have their license suspended or revoked.

C. ☐ The vehicle may be impounded.

D. ☐ All of the above are potential consequences for the owner of the vehicle.

9. What is the purpose of the practice driving tests required in California?

A. ☐ To ensure that drivers have a good understanding of the rules and regulations related to vehicle size and weight limits.

B. ☐ To assess the knowledge and skills of the driver.

C. ☐ Both A and B are correct.

D. ☐ To provide a way for the state to generate revenue.

10. Which of the following is NOT part of the practice driving test required in California?

    A. ☐ A written exam

    B. ☐ A practical driving test

    C. ☐ A physical fitness test

    D. ☐ A vision test

11. What is the maximum weight allowed for a single vehicle traveling on a county road in California?

    A. ☐ 12,000 pounds

    B. ☐ 14,000 pounds

    C. ☐ 16,000 pounds

    D. ☐ 18,000 pounds

12. What is the maximum weight allowed for a combination of vehicles, including a towing vehicle and trailer, traveling on a county road in California?

    A. ☐ 20,000 pounds

    B. ☐ 22,000 pounds

    C. ☐ 24,000 pounds

    D. ☐ 26,000 pounds

13. What is the maximum length allowed for a single vehicle traveling on a county road in California?

    A. ☐ 45 feet

    B. ☐ 50 feet

    C. ☐ 55 feet

    D. ☐ 60 feet

14. What is the maximum length allowed for a combination of vehicles, including a towing vehicle and trailer, traveling on a county road in California?

A. ☐ 65 feet

B. ☐ 70 feet

C. ☐ 75 feet

D. ☐ 80 feet

15. Are there any exceptions to the size and weight limits for vehicles in California based on the type of road being traveled on?

A. ☐ No, the size and weight limits are the same regardless of the type of road.

B. ☐ Yes, the size and weight limits may be increased for certain types of roads, such as highways.

C. ☐ Yes, the size and weight limits may be decreased for certain types of roads, such as residential streets.

D. ☐ Both B and C are correct.

Correct answers for vehicle size and weight limits exam 2

1. **C.** 20,000 pounds

2. **D.** 30,000 pounds

3. **B.** 36,000 pounds

4. **D.** 48,000 pounds

5. **C.** 75 feet

6. **B.** 90 feet

7. **B.** No, it is never legal to exceed the size and weight limits for a vehicle in California.

8. **D.** All of the above are potential consequences for the owner of the vehicle.

9. **C.** Both A and B are correct.

10. **C.** A physical fitness test

11. **B.** 14,000 pounds

12. **C.** 24,000 pounds

13. **D.** 60 feet

14. **A.** 65 feet

15. **A.** No, the size and weight limits are the same regardless of the type of road.

Vehicle size and weight limits exam 3

1. **What is the maximum gross vehicle weight rating (GVWR) for a Class 3 commercial vehicle?**

    A. ☐ 10,000 pounds

    B. ☐ 26,001-33,000 pounds

    C. ☐ 33,001-80,000 pounds

    D. ☐ Over 80,000 pounds

2. **What is the maximum allowable length for a single vehicle in the United States?**

    A. ☐ 45 feet

    B. ☐ 50 feet

    C. ☐ 75 feet

    D. ☐ No maximum length limit

3. **What is the maximum allowable length for a combination of vehicles in the United States?**

    A. ☐ 45 feet

    B. ☐ 50 feet

    C. ☐ 75 feet

    D. ☐ No maximum length limit

4. **What is the maximum allowable width for a single vehicle in the United States?**

    A. ☐ 8.5 feet

    B. ☐ 9.5 feet

    C. ☐ 10.5 feet

    D. ☐ No maximum width limit

5. What is the maximum allowable height for a single vehicle in the United States?

    A. ☐ 13.5 feet

    B. ☐ 14.5 feet

    C. ☐ 15.5 feet

    D. ☐ No maximum height limit

6. What is the maximum weight allowed for a tandem axle in most states?

    A. ☐ 34,000 pounds

    B. ☐ 36,000 pounds

    C. ☐ 38,000 pounds

    D. ☐ 40,000 pounds

7. What is the maximum weight allowed for a tridem axle in most states?

    A. ☐ 50,000 pounds

    B. ☐ 52,000 pounds

    C. ☐ 54,000 pounds

    D. ☐ 56,000 pounds

8. What is the maximum weight allowed for a quadridem axle in most states?

    A. ☐ 62,000 pounds

    B. ☐ 64,000 pounds

    C. ☐ 66,000 pounds

    D. ☐ 68,000 pounds

9. What is the maximum allowable number of axles for a single vehicle in the United States?

   A. ☐ 3 axles

   B. ☐ 4 axles

   C. ☐ 5 axles

   D. ☐ No maximum number of axles

10. What is the maximum weight allowed for a five-axle vehicle in most states?

   A. ☐ 80,000 pounds

   B. ☐ 82,000 pounds

   C. ☐ 84,000 pounds

   D. ☐ 86,000 pounds

11. What is the maximum length for a single vehicle in most states?

   A. ☐ 45 feet

   B. ☐ 50 feet

   C. ☐ 55 feet

   D. ☐ 60 feet

12. What is the maximum weight allowed for a single axle in most states?

   A. ☐ 20,000 pounds

   B. ☐ 22,000 pounds

   C. ☐ 24,000 pounds

   D. ☐ 26,000 pounds

13. **What is the maximum width for a vehicle without special permits in most states?**

   A. ☐ 8 feet

   B. ☐ 8.5 feet

   C. ☐ 9 feet

   D. ☐ 9.5 feet

14. **What is the maximum height for a vehicle in most states?**

   A. ☐ 13.5 feet

   B. ☐ 14 feet

   C. ☐ 14.5 feet

   D. ☐ 15 feet

15. **What is the maximum length for a combination vehicle (tractor-trailer) in most states?**

   A. ☐ 65 feet

   B. ☐ 70 feet

   C. ☐ 75 feet

   D. ☐ 80 feet

Correct answers for vehicle size and weight limits exam 3

1. **A.** 10,000 pounds
2. **C.** The maximum allowable length for a single vehicle in the United States is 75 feet.
3. **D.** There is no maximum length limit for a combination of vehicles in the United States.
4. **A.** The maximum allowable width for a single vehicle in the United States is 8.5 feet.
5. **A.** The maximum allowable height for a single vehicle in the United States is 13.5 feet.
6. **B.** 36,000 pounds
7. **C.** 54,000 pounds
8. **D.** 68,000 pounds
9. **B.** The maximum allowable number of axles for a single vehicle in the United States is 4 axles.
10. **D.** 86,000 pounds
11. **B.** 50 feet
12. **A.** 20,000 pounds
13. **B.** 8.5 feet
14. **D.** 15 feet
15. **B.** 70 feet

Vehicle size and weight limits exam 4

1. **What is the maximum gross vehicle weight (GVW) for a Class 3 vehicle?**

   A. ☐ 26,000 pounds

   B. ☐ 36,000 pounds

   C. ☐ 46,000 pounds

   D. ☐ 66,000 pounds

2. **What is the maximum width for a vehicle including its load?**

   A. ☐ 8 feet 6 inches

   B. ☐ 8 feet

   C. ☐ 8 feet 4 inches

   D. ☐ 7 feet 6 inches

3. **What is the maximum length for a semi-trailer truck including its load?**

   A. ☐ 48 feet

   B. ☐ 53 feet

   C. ☐ 63 feet

   D. ☐ 73 feet

4. **What is the maximum length for a single vehicle, including its load?**

   A. ☐ 40 feet

   B. ☐ 45 feet

   C. ☐ 50 feet

   D. ☐ 55 feet

5. **What is the maximum height for a vehicle including its load?**

A. ☐ 13 feet 6 inches

B. ☐ 13 feet

C. ☐ 14 feet

D. ☐ 14 feet 6 inches

6. **What is the maximum weight limit for a single axle on a vehicle?**

A. ☐ 12,000 pounds

B. ☐ 14,000 pounds

C. ☐ 16,000 pounds

D. ☐ 18,000 pounds

7. **What is the maximum weight limit for a tandem axle on a vehicle?**

A. ☐ 24,000 pounds

B. ☐ 28,000 pounds

C. ☐ 32,000 pounds

D. ☐ 36,000 pounds

8. **What is the maximum weight limit for a tridem axle on a vehicle?**

A. ☐ 36,000 pounds

B. ☐ 42,000 pounds

C. ☐ 48,000 pounds

D. ☐ 54,000 pounds

9. What is the maximum weight limit for a quadem axle on a vehicle?

A. ☐ 48,000 pounds

B. ☐ 54,000 pounds

C. ☐ 60,000 pounds

D. ☐ 66,000 pounds

10. What is the maximum weight limit for a gross combination weight rating (GCWR)?

A. ☐ 80,000 pounds

B. ☐ 90,000 pounds

C. ☐ 100,000 pounds

D. ☐ 110,000 pounds

11. What is the maximum weight limit for a single rear axle on a vehicle?

A. ☐ 10,000 pounds

B. ☐ 12,000 pounds

C. ☐ 14,000 pounds

D. ☐ 16,000 pounds

12. What is the maximum weight limit for a tandem rear axle on a vehicle?

A. ☐ 20,000 pounds

B. ☐ 24,000 pounds

C. ☐ 28,000 pounds

D. ☐ 32,000 pounds

13. What is the maximum weight limit for a tridem rear axle on a vehicle?

A. ☐ 30,000 pounds

B. ☐ 36,000 pounds

C. ☐ 42,000 pounds

D. ☐ 48,000 pounds

14. What is the maximum weight limit for a quadem rear axle on a vehicle?

A. ☐ 40,000 pounds

B. ☐ 46,000 pounds

C. ☐ 52,000 pounds

D. ☐ 58,000 pounds

15. What is the maximum weight limit for a gross vehicle weight (GVW)?

A. ☐ 60,000 pounds

B. ☐ 70,000 pounds

C. ☐ 80,000 pounds

D. ☐ 90,000 pounds

Correct answers for vehicle size and weight limits exam 4

1. **C.** 46,000 pounds
2. **A.** 8 feet 6 inches
3. **B.** 53 feet
4. **C.** 50 feet
5. **A.** 13 feet 6 inches
6. **C.** 16,000 pounds
7. **D.** 36,000 pounds
8. **C.** 48,000 pounds
9. **D.** 66,000 pounds
10. **C.** 100,000 pounds
11. **B.** 12,000 pounds
12. **D.** 32,000 pounds
13. **C.** 42,000 pounds
14. **D.** 58,000 pounds
15. **C.** 80,000 pounds

Vehicle size and weight limits exam 5

1. **What is the maximum weight limit for a single front axle on a vehicle?**

   A. ☐ 6,000 pounds

   B. ☐ 8,000 pounds

   C. ☐ 10,000 pounds

   D. ☐ 12,000 pounds

2. **What is the maximum weight limit for a tandem front axle on a vehicle?**

   A. ☐ 16,000 pounds

   B. ☐ 18,000 pounds

   C. ☐ 20,000 pounds

   D. ☐ 22,000 pounds

3. **What is the maximum weight limit for a tridem front axle on a vehicle?**

   A. ☐ 24,000 pounds

   B. ☐ 26,000 pounds

   C. ☐ 28,000 pounds

   D. ☐ 30,000 pounds

4. **What is the maximum weight limit for a quadem front axle on a vehicle?**

   A. ☐ 32,000 pounds

   B. ☐ 34,000 pounds

   C. ☐ 36,000 pounds

   D. ☐ 38,000 pounds

5. What is the maximum weight limit for a gross combination weight rating (GCWR) of a truck-tractor and semi-trailer?

    A. ☐ 80,000 pounds

    B. ☐ 90,000 pounds

    C. ☐ 100,000 pounds

    D. ☐ 110,000 pounds

6. What is the maximum weight limit for a gross combination weight rating (GCWR) of a truck-tractor and two trailers?

    A. ☐ 90,000 pounds

    B. ☐ 100,000 pounds

    C. ☐ 110,000 pounds

    D. ☐ 120,000 pounds

7. What is the maximum weight limit for a gross combination weight rating (GCWR) of a truck-tractor and three trailers?

    A. ☐ 100,000 pounds

    B. ☐ 110,000 pounds

    C. ☐ 120,000 pounds

    D. ☐ 130,000 pounds

8. What is the maximum weight limit for a gross combination weight rating (GCWR) of a truck-tractor and four trailers?

    A. ☐ 110,000 pounds

    B. ☐ 120,000 pounds

    C. ☐ 130,000 pounds

    D. ☐ 140,000 pounds

9. What is the maximum weight limit for a gross combination weight rating (GCWR) of a truck-tractor and five trailers?

    A. ☐ 120,000 pounds

    B. ☐ 130,000 pounds

    C. ☐ 140,000 pounds

    D. ☐ 150,000 pounds

10. What is the maximum weight limit for a gross combination weight rating (GCWR) of a truck-tractor and six trailers?

    A. ☐ 130,000 pounds

    B. ☐ 140,000 pounds

    C. ☐ 150,000 pounds

    D. ☐ 160,000 pounds

11. What is the maximum weight limit for a single rear axle on a vehicle in a rural area?

    A. ☐ 10,000 pounds

    B. ☐ 12,000 pounds

    C. ☐ 14,000 pounds

    D. ☐ 16,000 pounds

12. What is the maximum weight limit for a tandem rear axle on a vehicle in a rural area?

    A. ☐ 20,000 pounds

    B. ☐ 22,000 pounds

    C. ☐ 24,000 pounds

    D. ☐ 26,000 pounds

13. What is the maximum weight limit for a tridem rear axle on a vehicle in a rural area?

    A. ☐ 28,000 pounds

    B. ☐ 30,000 pounds

    C. ☐ 32,000 pounds

    D. ☐ 34,000 pounds

14. What is the maximum weight limit for a quadem rear axle on a vehicle in a rural area?

    A. ☐ 36,000 pounds

    B. ☐ 38,000 pounds

    C. ☐ 40,000 pounds

    D. ☐ 42,000 pounds

15. What is the maximum weight limit for a gross vehicle weight (GVW) in a rural area?

    A. ☐ 44,000 pounds

    B. ☐ 46,000 pounds

    C. ☐ 48,000 pounds

    D. ☐ 50,000 pounds

Correct answers for vehicle size and weight limits exam 5

1. **C.** 10,000 pounds
2. **A.** 16,000 pounds
3. **D.** 30,000 pounds
4. **C.** 36,000 pounds
5. **C.** 100,000 pounds
6. **B.** 100,000 pounds
7. **C.** 120,000 pounds
8. **D.** 140,000 pounds
9. **B.** 130,000 pounds
10. **C.** 150,000 pounds
11. **B.** 12,000 pounds
12. **C.** 24,000 pounds
13. **D.** 34,000 pounds
14. **A.** 36,000 pounds
15. **C.** 48,000 pounds

Public transportation

Public transportation is an essential part of daily life in California, providing residents and visitors with a reliable and convenient way to get around the state. From buses and trains to ferries and light rail systems, there are many options for public transportation in California. However, for those who prefer to drive, obtaining a driver's license is a necessary step.

One important aspect of obtaining a driver's license in California is passing a driving test. These tests are designed to ensure that new drivers have the knowledge and skills necessary to operate a vehicle safely on the road. In this chapter, we will explore the various types of driving tests available in California, as well as the steps you need to take in order to prepare for and successfully pass these tests.

There are several types of driving tests that you may be required to take in California, depending on your age and driving experience. The most common types of driving tests are the learner's permit test, the driver's license test, and the road test.

The learner's permit test is the first step in the process of obtaining a driver's license. This test is typically taken by individuals who are at least 15 years old and who have never held a driver's license before. The learner's permit test covers the basic rules of the road and safe driving practices, as well as any local traffic laws.

The driver's license test is a more comprehensive test that is required for individuals who are seeking to upgrade their learner's permit to a full driver's license. This test covers a wider range of topics, including road signs, traffic laws, and defensive driving techniques.

Finally, the road test is a practical test that is designed to assess your driving skills and abilities. During the road test, you will be asked to demonstrate your ability to safely operate a vehicle, including tasks such as starting and stopping, turning, and parallel parking.

In order to prepare for these driving tests, it is important to study the California Driver Handbook, which covers all of the material that you will be tested on. You may also want to consider taking a driver's education course or practicing with a licensed driver who has at least three years of driving experience.

In addition to the traditional driving tests, there are also a number of specialized driving tests that may be required in certain circumstances. For example, individuals who are seeking to obtain a commercial driver's license (CDL) will be required to take a separate set of tests that cover the specific skills and knowledge required to operate a commercial vehicle.

Regardless of the type of driving test you are taking, it is important to arrive at the testing location on time and to bring all necessary documents and materials with you. You should also be well-rested and mentally prepared for the test, as your ability to concentrate and make quick decisions will be critical to your success.

With the right preparation and practice, you can confidently take on the challenge of the California driving tests and earn your driver's license. In the following chapters, we will delve deeper into the specifics of each type of driving test, as well as provide tips and strategies for success. So, let's begin our journey to becoming a licensed driver in California.

For training purposes, you can mark the ▢ symbol next to what you think is the correct answer: Once you have chosen the correct answer, use a pencil or pen to mark the ▢ symbol next to that answer.

Public transportation exam

1. **What should you do if you are approaching a pedestrian who is using a white cane or a guide dog?**

   A. ☐ Honk your horn to alert them to your presence

   B. ☐ Proceed with caution and give the pedestrian plenty of space

   C. ☐ Speed up to get past them quickly

   D. ☐ Ignore the pedestrian and continue driving as normal

2. **What should you do if you are driving and come across a school bus that is stopped and has its red lights flashing?**

   A. ☐ Pass the school bus on the right side

   B. ☐ Wait until the red lights stop flashing before proceeding

   C. ☐ Pass the school bus on the left side

   D. ☐ Stop your vehicle at least 20 feet away from the bus

3. **What is the maximum number of passengers allowed on a city bus?**

   A. ☐ 15

   B. ☐ 20

   C. ☐ 25

   D. ☐ 30

4. **You are driving on a highway and see an emergency vehicle approaching from the opposite direction with its sirens and lights on. You should:**

   A. ☐ Pull over to the right side of the road and stop

   B. ☐ Continue driving and let the emergency vehicle pass

   C. ☐ Pull over to the left side of the road and stop

   D. ☐ Speed up to get out of the way of the emergency vehicle

5. **Which of the following is NOT a common form of public transportation?**

A. ☐ Trains

B. ☐ Buses

C. ☐ Taxis

D. ☐ Boats

6. **You are driving on a road with a speed limit of 35 mph. You see a school crossing ahead with children crossing the street. You should:**

A. ☐ Slow down and proceed with caution

B. ☐ Proceed at the same speed, but be prepared to stop if necessary

C. ☐ Speed up to get through the crossing as quickly as possible

D. ☐ Honk your horn to signal the children to get out of the way

7. **What is the maximum speed limit for a city bus on a residential street?**

A. ☐ 25 mph

B. ☐ 35 mph

C. ☐ 45 mph

D. ☐ 55 mph

8. **When driving a public transportation vehicle, which of the following is NOT a necessary safety precaution?**

A. ☐ Wearing a seatbelt

B. ☐ Obeying traffic laws

C. ☐ Checking mirrors frequently

D. ☐ Using a cell phone while driving

9. **What should you do if you are involved in a collision while driving a public transportation vehicle?**

A. ☐ Leave the scene of the accident

B. ☐ Try to fix any damage yourself

C. ☐ Wait for the police to arrive

D. ☐ Ask the passengers if they are okay

10. **You are driving on a road with a speed limit of 25 mph. You see a pedestrian crossing the street at a crosswalk. You should:**

A. ☐ Speed up to get past the pedestrian as quickly as possible

B. ☐ Slow down and give the pedestrian plenty of room

C. ☐ Honk your horn to signal the pedestrian to get out of the way

D. ☐ Proceed with caution and be prepared to stop if necessary

11. **What is the maximum number of hours that a public transportation driver is allowed to work in one day?**

A. ☐ 8 hours

B. ☐ 10 hours

C. ☐ 12 hours

D. ☐ 14 hours

12. **What should you do if a passenger asks to be let off at a location that is not a designated stop?**

A. ☐ Allow the passenger to get off at the requested location

B. ☐ Refuse to let the passenger off

C. ☐ Explain to the passenger that the requested location is not a designated stop

D. ☐ Ask the passenger to pay an additional fee for the deviation from the route

13. **What should you do if a passenger attempts to board the public transportation vehicle without paying the fare?**

A. ☐ Allow the passenger to ride for free

B. ☐ Refuse to let the passenger board the vehicle

C. ☐ Ask the passenger to pay the fare before boarding

D. ☐ Call the police for assistance

14. **What is the appropriate distance to maintain from the vehicle in front of you while driving a bus or other large vehicle?**

A. ☐ One car length for every 10 mph of speed

B. ☐ Two car lengths for every 10 mph of speed

C. ☐ Three car lengths for every 10 mph of speed

D. ☐ Four car lengths for every 10 mph of speed

15. **What should you do when approaching a railroad crossing with active warning signals?**

A. ☐ Proceed through the crossing as quickly as possible

B. ☐ Stop at least 15 feet from the nearest rail and remain stopped until the warning signals have ceased

C. ☐ Proceed through the crossing as long as there are no trains in sight

D. ☐ Turn around and take a different route

Correct answers for public transportation exam

1. **B.** Proceed with caution and give the pedestrian plenty of space
2. **D.** Stop your vehicle at least 20 feet away from the bus
3. **C.** 25
4. **A.** Pull over to the right side of the road and stop
5. **D.** Boats
6. **A.** Slow down and proceed with caution
7. **A.** 25 mph
8. **D.** Using a cell phone while driving
9. **C.** Wait for the police to arrive
10. **D.** Proceed with caution and be prepared to stop if necessary
11. **C.** 12 hours
12. **C.** Explain to the passenger that the requested location is not a designated stop
13. **C.** Ask the passenger to pay the fare before boarding
14. **B.** Two car lengths for every 10 mph of speed
15. **B.** Stop at least 15 feet from the nearest rail and remain stopped until the warning signals have ceased

Public transportation exam 2

1. **You are driving on a road with a speed limit of 35 mph. You see a pedestrian crossing the street at a crosswalk. You should:**

   A. ☐ Speed up to get past the pedestrian as quickly as possible

   B. ☐ Slow down and give the pedestrian plenty of room

   C. ☐ Honk your horn to signal the pedestrian to get out of the way

   D. ☐ Proceed with caution and be prepared to stop if necessary

2. **You are driving on a highway and see a vehicle ahead of you with its hazard lights on. You should:**

   A. ☐ Speed up to get around the vehicle as quickly as possible

   B. ☐ Slow down and proceed with caution

   C. ☐ Honk your horn to signal the driver to move out of the way

   D. ☐ Move into the left lane to pass the vehicle

3. **You are driving on a road with a speed limit of 45 mph. You see a school bus stopped on the side of the road with its red lights flashing. You should:**

   A. ☐ Pass the school bus on the right side

   B. ☐ Wait until the red lights stop flashing before proceeding

   C. ☐ Pass the school bus on the left side

   D. ☐ Stop your vehicle at least 20 feet away from the bus

4. **When driving a bus or other large vehicle, what is the correct procedure for making a right turn at an intersection?**

   A. ☐ Signal, then turn wide to the left to allow for a wider turning radius

   B. ☐ Signal, then turn directly into the intersection

   C. ☐ Signal, then turn wide to the right to allow for a wider turning radius

   D. ☐ Signal, then make a sharp turn into the intersection

5. You are driving on a road with a speed limit of 55 mph. You see a pedestrian walking on the side of the road. You should:

  A. ☐ Speed up to get past the pedestrian as quickly as possible

  B. ☐ Slow down and give the pedestrian plenty of room

  C. ☐ Honk your horn to signal the pedestrian to get out of the way

  D. ☐ Proceed with caution and be prepared to stop if necessary

6. You are driving on a highway and come across a railway crossing with no gates or flashing lights. You should:

  A. ☐ Proceed through the crossing without stopping

  B. ☐ Slow down and proceed with caution

  C. ☐ Stop your vehicle at least 15 feet from the nearest rail

  D. ☐ Honk your horn to warn any approaching trains

7. You are driving on a road with a speed limit of 65 mph. You see a blind pedestrian at a marked crosswalk. You should:

  A. ☐ Speed up to get past the pedestrian as quickly as possible

  B. ☐ Slow down and proceed with caution

  C. ☐ Honk your horn to signal the pedestrian to get out of the way

  D. ☐ Proceed with caution and be prepared to stop if necessary

8. You are driving on a highway and come to a construction zone. You see a flagger waving a red flag at you. You should:

  A. ☐ Ignore the flagger and continue driving

  B. ☐ Proceed with caution and follow the flagger's instructions

  C. ☐ Stop your vehicle and wait for further instructions

  D. ☐ Turn around and find an alternate route

9. You are driving on a road with a speed limit of 75 mph. You see a pedestrian crossing the street at a crosswalk. You should:

    A. ☐ Speed up to get past the pedestrian as quickly as possible

    B. ☐ Slow down and give the pedestrian plenty of room

    C. ☐ Honk your horn to signal the pedestrian to get out of the way

    D. ☐ Proceed with caution and be prepared to stop if necessary

10. What should you do if a tire on your bus or other large vehicle blows out while driving?

    A. ☐ Continue driving on the rim until you can safely pull over

    B. ☐ Brake hard and come to a stop as quickly as possible

    C. ☐ Ease off the gas pedal and slowly pull over to the side of the road

    D. ☐ Steer sharply in the direction of the blown-out tire to correct your course

11. How should you react if a pedestrian is crossing the street in a marked crosswalk while you are driving a bus or other large vehicle?

    A. ☐ Speed up to get through the crosswalk before the pedestrian

    B. ☐ Honk your horn to alert the pedestrian to your presence

    C. ☐ Stop and wait for the pedestrian to fully cross the street

    D. ☐ Proceed through the crosswalk, but slow down to allow the pedestrian to pass safely

12. When driving a bus or other large vehicle, what is the correct procedure for making a left turn at an intersection?

    A. ☐ Signal, then turn wide to the right to allow for a wider turning radius

    B. ☐ Signal, then turn directly into the intersection

    C. ☐ Signal, then turn wide to the left to allow for a wider turning radius

    D. ☐ Signal, then make a sharp turn into the intersection

13. What should you do if you are involved in a collision while driving a bus or other large vehicle?

    A. ☐ Leave the scene as quickly as possible

    B. ☐ Check for injuries and call for medical assistance if necessary

    C. ☐ Exchange information with the other driver and file a report with the authorities

    D. ☐ Try to hide any damage to the vehicle

14. How should you react if a traffic light turns red while you are driving a bus or other large vehicle?

    A. ☐ Proceed through the intersection if there is no cross traffic

    B. ☐ Stop at the line and wait for the light to turn green

    C. ☐ Speed up to get through the intersection before the light turns red

    D. ☐ Ignore the red light and continue driving

15. What should you do if you encounter a school bus that is stopped and displaying flashing red lights while driving a bus or other large vehicle?

    A. ☐ Proceed with caution and be prepared to stop

    B. ☐ Pass the school bus at a safe speed

    C. ☐ Stop at least 20 feet from the school bus and wait until the red lights are no longer flashing before proceeding

    D. ☐ Ignore the school bus and continue driving

Correct answers for public transportation exam 2

1. **D.** Proceed with caution and be prepared to stop if necessary
2. **B.** Slow down and proceed with caution
3. **D.** Stop your vehicle at least 20 feet away from the bus
4. **C.** Signal, then turn wide to the right to allow for a wider turning radius
5. **B.** Slow down and give the pedestrian plenty of room
6. **B.** Slow down and proceed with caution
7. **B.** Slow down and proceed with caution
8. **B.** Proceed with caution and follow the flagger's instructions
9. **D.** Proceed with caution and be prepared to stop if necessary
10. **C.** Ease off the gas pedal and slowly pull over to the side of the road
11. **C.** Stop and wait for the pedestrian to fully cross the street
12. **B.** Signal, then turn directly into the intersection
13. **B.** Check for injuries and call for medical assistance if necessary
14. **B.** Stop at the line and wait for the light to turn green
15. **C.** Stop at least 20 feet from the school bus and wait until the red lights are no longer flashing before proceeding

Public transportation exam 3

1. **When driving a bus, what should you do when approaching a pedestrian in a crosswalk?**

   A. ☐ Slow down and be prepared to stop

   B. ☐ Continue driving at the same speed

   C. ☐ Honk the horn to signal the pedestrian to move out of the way

   D. ☐ Swerve around the pedestrian to avoid stopping

2. **When driving a train, what should you do when approaching a grade crossing with active warning devices?**

   A. ☐ Proceed at the posted speed limit

   B. ☐ Stop and wait for the warning devices to turn off

   C. ☐ Proceed with caution and be prepared to stop if necessary

   D. ☐ Ignore the warning devices and continue through the crossing

3. **When driving a taxi, what should you do if a passenger becomes disruptive or behaves aggressively?**

   A. ☐ Ignore the behavior and continue driving

   B. ☐ Pull over and ask the passenger to leave the vehicle

   C. ☐ Attempt to calm the passenger down by talking to them

   D. ☐ Call the police for assistance

4. **When driving a shuttle bus, what should you do when loading or unloading passengers with mobility devices?**

   A. ☐ Ask the passengers to move their mobility devices out of the way

   B. ☐ Ignore the passengers and continue loading or unloading other passengers

   C. ☐ Assist the passengers in safely boarding or exiting the bus

   D. ☐ Deny service to the passengers with mobility devices

5. When driving a school bus, what should you do when stopped at a railroad crossing with flashing red lights and a lowered crossing gate?

A. ☐ Proceed through the crossing as quickly as possible

B. ☐ Ignore the warning signals and continue driving

C. ☐ Stop at least 15 feet from the nearest rail and wait for the gates to rise

D. ☐ Stop the bus and allow passengers to disembark before crossing the tracks

6. When driving a transit bus, what should you do when a passenger signals for a stop?

A. ☐ Ignore the signal and continue driving to the next scheduled stop

B. ☐ Pull over to the side of the road and let the passenger off

C. ☐ Ask the passenger to pay the fare before allowing them to disembark

D. ☐ Tell the passenger that they need to wait until the next scheduled stop

7. You are driving on a road with a speed limit of 70 mph. You see a school bus stopped on the side of the road with its red lights flashing. You should:

A. ☐ Pass the school bus on the right side

B. ☐ Wait until the red lights stop flashing before proceeding

C. ☐ Pass the school bus on the left side

D. ☐ Stop your vehicle at least 20 feet away from the bus

8. You are driving on a two-lane road and there is a bicycle in the lane next to you. You should:

A. ☐ Speed up and pass the bicycle as quickly as possible

B. ☐ Honk your horn to signal the bicycle to move out of the way

C. ☐ Slow down and leave plenty of room between your vehicle and the bicycle

D. ☐ Move over into the bike lane to pass the bicycle

9. **You are driving on a highway and see a car stopped on the shoulder with its hazard lights on. You should:**

A. ☐ Speed up to get around the car as quickly as possible

B. ☐ Slow down and proceed with caution

C. ☐ Honk your horn to signal the driver to move out of the way

D. ☐ Move into the left lane to pass the car

10. **You are driving on a road with a speed limit of 50 mph. You see a pedestrian crossing the street at a crosswalk. You should:**

A. ☐ Speed up to get past the pedestrian as quickly as possible

B. ☐ Slow down and give the pedestrian plenty of room

C. ☐ Honk your horn to signal the pedestrian to get out of the way

D. ☐ Proceed with caution and be prepared to stop if necessary

11. **You are driving on a highway and come across a railway crossing with gates and flashing lights. You should:**

A. ☐ Proceed through the crossing without stopping

B. ☐ Slow down and proceed with caution

C. ☐ Stop your vehicle at least 15 feet from the nearest rail

D. ☐ Honk your horn to warn any approaching trains

12. **You are driving on a two-lane road and there is a motorcycle in the lane next to you. You should:**

A. ☐ Speed up and pass the motorcycle as quickly as possible

B. ☐ Honk your horn to signal the motorcycle to move out of the way

C. ☐ Slow down and leave plenty of room between your vehicle and the motorcycle

D. ☐ Move over into the bike lane to pass the motorcycle

13. You are driving on a road with a speed limit of 60 mph. You see a pedestrian walking on the side of the road. You should:

A. ☐ Speed up to get past the pedestrian as quickly as possible

B. ☐ Slow down and give the pedestrian plenty of room

C. ☐ Honk your horn to signal the pedestrian to get out of the way

D. ☐ Proceed with caution and be prepared to stop if necessary

14. You are driving on a highway and come to a construction zone. You see a flagger waving a yellow flag at you. You should:

A. ☐ Ignore the flagger and continue driving

B. ☐ Proceed with caution and follow the flagger's instructions

C. ☐ Stop your vehicle and wait for further instructions

D. ☐ Turn around and find an alternate route

15. You are driving on a road with a speed limit of 70 mph. You see a pedestrian crossing the street at a crosswalk. You should:

A. ☐ Speed up to get past the pedestrian as quickly as possible

B. ☐ Slow down and give the pedestrian plenty of room

C. ☐ Honk your horn to signal the pedestrian to get out of the way

Correct answers for public transportation exam 3

1. **A.** Slow down and be prepared to stop

2. **C.** Proceed with caution and be prepared to stop if necessary

3. **B.** Pull over and ask the passenger to leave the vehicle

4. **C.** Slow down and leave plenty of room between your vehicle and the motorcycle

5. **C.** Stop at least 15 feet from the nearest rail and wait for the gates to rise

6. **B.** Pull over to the side of the road and let the passenger off

7. **D.** Stop your vehicle at least 20 feet away from the bus

8. **C.** Slow down and leave plenty of room between your vehicle and the bicycle

9. **B.** Slow down and proceed with caution

10. **D.** Proceed with caution and be prepared to stop if necessary

11. **C.** Stop your vehicle at least 15 feet from the nearest rail

12. **C.** Slow down and leave plenty of room between your vehicle and the motorcycle

13. **B.** Slow down and give the pedestrian plenty of room

14. **B.** Proceed with caution and follow the flagger's instructions

15. **B.** Slow down and give the pedestrian plenty of room

Public transportation exam 4

1. **When driving a paratransit van, what should you do when a passenger asks to be taken to a location that is outside of your service area?**

   A. ☐ Agree to take the passenger to their desired destination and charge them an additional fee

   B. ☐ Refuse to take the passenger to their destination and ask them to find another form of transportation

   C. ☐ Check with your dispatch to see if an exception can be made and inform the passenger of the decision

   D. ☐ Ignore the request and continue driving to the next scheduled pick-up

2. **When driving a coach bus, what should you do when encountering a traffic jam or construction on your route?**

   A. ☐ Drive on the shoulder or other designated emergency lane to bypass the congestion

   B. ☐ Honk the horn and try to force your way through the traffic

   C. ☐ Follow the detour route provided by the authorities or your dispatch

   D. ☐ Pull over to the side of the road and wait for the congestion to clear

3. **When driving a ferry, what should you do when encountering rough seas or inclement weather?**

   A. ☐ Ignore the conditions and continue on your usual route

   B. ☐ Reduce speed and take appropriate precautions to ensure the safety of your passengers

   C. ☐ Turn back to the starting point and cancel the trip

   D. ☐ Attempt to outrun the adverse conditions

4. When should a bus driver use the emergency brake?

A. ☐ When the bus is approaching a stop

B. ☐ When a passenger becomes unruly

C. ☐ When the bus is entering a curve

D. ☐ When there is an unexpected obstacle in the road

5. What is the purpose of a bus route?

A. ☐ To connect remote areas to major cities

B. ☐ To transport people within a city or town

C. ☐ To transport goods across long distances

D. ☐ To provide transportation for tourists

6. How should a bus driver communicate with passengers who are deaf or hard of hearing?

A. ☐ Use hand gestures to communicate

B. ☐ Use written notes to communicate

C. ☐ Use a microphone to amplify their voice

D. ☐ Use a phone or text message to communicate

7. When should a bus driver use the turn signals?

A. ☐ When changing lanes

B. ☐ When turning at an intersection

C. ☐ When entering or exiting a highway

D. ☐ All of the above

8. **What should a bus driver do if a passenger becomes ill on the bus?**

A. ☐ Ask the passenger to leave the bus

B. ☐ Provide the passenger with medical assistance

C. ☐ Continue on the route without stopping

D. ☐ Call the police

9. **How should a bus driver handle a passenger who is being disruptive or causing a disturbance on the bus?**

A. ☐ Ignore the behavior and continue on the route

B. ☐ Ask the passenger to leave the bus

C. ☐ Call the police

D. ☐ Speak to the passenger in a calm and respectful manner

10. **What should a bus driver do if the bus breaks down while on the route?**

A. ☐ Continue on the route and hope the problem resolves itself

B. ☐ Call for a replacement bus

C. ☐ Have the passengers exit the bus and wait for a replacement

D. ☐ Attempt to fix the problem themselves

11. **How should a bus driver handle a passenger who is smoking on the bus?**

A. ☐ Ignore the behavior and continue on the route

B. ☐ Ask the passenger to stop smoking

C. ☐ Ask the passenger to leave the bus

D. ☐ Call the police

12. How should a bus driver handle a passenger who is intoxicated or under the influence of drugs?

A. ☐ Ignore the behavior and continue on the route

B. ☐ Ask the passenger to leave the bus

C. ☐ Call the police

D. ☐ Provide the passenger with medical assistance

13. What should a bus driver do if they are involved in a collision while on the route?

A. ☐ Continue on the route without stopping

B. ☐ Stop the bus and check for injuries

C. ☐ Leave the scene of the accident

D. ☐ Call the police and wait for their arrival

14. What should you do if you miss your bus or train?

A. ☐ Wait at the stop for the next one

B. ☐ Flag down a taxi

C. ☐ Walk to your destination

D. ☐ Run after the vehicle

15. What is the proper way to signal to the driver that you want to get off at the next stop?

A. ☐ Ring the bell or press the stop button

B. ☐ Yell "stop"

C. ☐ Stand up and wave your arms

D. ☐ Ignore the stop and get off at the next one

Correct answers for public transportation exam 4

1. **C.** Check with your dispatch to see if an exception can be made and inform the passenger of the decision

2. **C.** Follow the detour route provided by the authorities or your dispatch

3. **B.** Reduce speed and take appropriate precautions to ensure the safety of your passengers

4. **D.** (Airplane)

5. **B.** (To transport people within a city or town)

6. **C.** Use a microphone to amplify their voice. It is important for bus drivers to communicate effectively with all passengers, including those who are deaf or hard of hearing. Using a microphone to amplify the voice is an effective way to ensure that all passengers can hear the information being provided by the bus driver.

7. **D.** All of the above. Bus drivers should use the turn signals any time they are changing lanes, turning at an intersection, or entering or exiting a highway. This helps to communicate the bus driver's intentions to other drivers and helps to prevent accidents.

8. **B.** Provide the passenger with medical assistance. If a passenger becomes ill on the bus, it is the responsibility of the bus driver to provide them with medical assistance. This may include calling for emergency medical services if the situation is serious.

9. **D.** Speak to the passenger in a calm and respectful manner. It is important for bus drivers to maintain control of the bus and to ensure that all passengers are behaving appropriately. If a passenger is being disruptive or causing a disturbance, the bus driver should speak to them in a calm and respectful manner and ask them to stop the behavior.

10. **B.** Call for a replacement bus. If the bus breaks down while on the route, it is the responsibility of the bus driver to call for a replacement bus to continue the route. The bus driver should not try to fix the problem themselves or have the passengers exit the bus.

11. **B.** Ask the passenger to stop smoking. Smoking is not allowed on public buses, and bus drivers should ask any passengers who are smoking to stop.

12. **B.** Ask the passenger to leave the bus. It is the responsibility of the bus driver to ensure the safety and well-being of all passengers on the bus. If a passenger is intoxicated or under the influence of drugs, they may pose a risk to themselves or others and should be asked to leave the bus.

13. **B.** Stop the bus and check for injuries. If the bus is involved in a collision, the driver should stop the bus and check for injuries. If anyone is injured, the bus driver should call for emergency

medical services. The bus driver should not leave the scene of the accident or continue on the route.

14. A. Wait at the stop for the next one

15. A. Ring the bell or press the stop button

Public transportation exam 5

1. **Which of the following is NOT a common type of public transportation in urban areas?**

A. ☐ Subway

B. ☐ Bus

C. ☐ Tram

D. ☐ Helicopter

2. **How should you behave on public transportation?**

A. ☐ Talk loudly on your phone or listen to music without headphones

B. ☐ Eat or drink

C. ☐ Take up more than one seat with your belongings

D. ☐ Respect the personal space and quiet of other passengers

3. **What is the main difference between a light rail and a heavy rail system?**

A. ☐ Light rail systems are powered by electricity, while heavy rail systems are powered by diesel

B. ☐ Light rail systems are smaller and operate on less crowded routes, while heavy rail systems are larger and operate on more crowded routes

C. ☐ Light rail systems operate above ground, while heavy rail systems operate underground

D. ☐ Light rail systems are faster than heavy rail systems

4. **What is the main advantage of a ferry system over other types of public transportation?**

A. ☐ It is faster

B. ☐ It is cheaper

C. ☐ It is more environmentally friendly

D. ☐ It allows for transportation across bodies of water

5. **What is the main purpose of a subway system?**

A. ☐ To connect remote areas to major cities

B. ☐ To transport people within a city or town

C. ☐ To transport goods across long distances

D. ☐ To provide transportation for tourists

6. **What should you do if you see suspicious behavior or a safety hazard on a bus or train?**

A. ☐ Ignore it and hope it goes away

B. ☐ Confront the person yourself

C. ☐ Alert the driver or a transportation worker

D. ☐ Tweet about it

7. **What is the main advantage of using public transportation over driving a personal vehicle?**

A. ☐ It is faster

B. ☐ It is cheaper

C. ☐ It is more environmentally friendly

D. ☐ It is safer

8. **Which of the following is NOT a common type of public transportation?**

A. ☐ Subway

B. ☐ Bus

C. ☐ Tram

D. ☐ Airplane

9. **How do most public transportation systems charge for fares?**

A. ☐ By the mile traveled

B. ☐ By the number of stops made

C. ☐ By the time spent on the vehicle

D. ☐ By the number of passengers on the vehicle

10. **What type of vehicle is typically used for public transportation in cities?**

A. ☐ Bus

B. ☐ Train

C. ☐ Boat

D. ☐ Plane

11. **What is the main advantage of a bike-sharing system over traditional public transportation?**

A. ☐ It is faster

B. ☐ It is cheaper

C. ☐ It is more environmentally friendly

D. ☐ It allows for more personalized routes

12. **Which of the following is NOT a common method of payment for public transportation fares?**

A. ☐ Cash

B. ☐ Credit card

C. ☐ Smart card

D. ☐ PayPal

13. What is the main advantage of using a public transportation pass over paying for individual fares?

A. It is faster

B. ☐ It is cheaper

C. ☐ It is more convenient

D. ☐ It is safer

14. What is the main purpose of a bus route?

A. ☐ To connect remote areas to major cities

B. ☐ To transport people within a city or town

C. ☐ To transport goods across long distances

D. ☐ To provide transportation for tourists

15. Which of the following is NOT a common type of public transportation in rural areas?

A. ☐ Bus

B. ☐ Train

C. ☐ Boat

D. ☐ Plane

Correct answers for public transportation exam 5

1. **D.** (Helicopter)
2. **D.** Respect the personal space and quiet of other passengers
3. **B.** (Light rail systems are smaller and operate on less crowded routes, while heavy rail systems are larger and operate on more crowded routes)
4. **D.** (It allows for transportation across bodies of water)
5. **B.** (To transport people within a city or town)
6. **C.** Alert the driver or a transportation worker
7. **C.** (It is more environmentally friendly)
8. **D.** (Airplane)
9. **D.** (By the number of passengers on the vehicle)
10. **A.** (Bus)
11. **C.** (It is more environmentally friendly)
12. **D.** (PayPal)
13. **B.** (It is cheaper)
14. **B.** (To transport people within a city or town)
15. **D.** (Plane)

Conclusion

In conclusion, it is essential for all drivers in California to have a thorough understanding of the various topics covered in the practice driving tests. From traffic laws and signs, to vehicle control and safety, to alcohol and drugs, to vehicle equipment and maintenance, to sharing the road and transportation of hazardous materials, to vehicle registration and insurance, to emergencies, to vehicle size and weight limits, and to public transportation, these are all critical components of safe and responsible driving.

It is important to note that the practice driving tests are designed to evaluate a driver's knowledge and understanding of these various topics, and to ensure that they are prepared and capable of safely operating a vehicle on the roads of California. By thoroughly studying and preparing for the practice driving tests, drivers can increase their chances of success and reduce the risk of accidents and injuries on the road.

In addition to the knowledge and skills required to pass the practice driving tests, it is also important for drivers to be aware of the various laws and regulations that apply to driving in California. These include laws related to speed limits, seat belt use, cell phone use, and other important safety measures. By following these laws and regulations, drivers can help to ensure their own safety and the safety of others on the road.

Overall, the practice driving tests in California play a vital role in promoting safe and responsible driving, and it is important for all drivers to take them seriously and to be fully prepared before taking the tests. By demonstrating a thorough understanding of the various topics covered in the tests, and by following all applicable laws and regulations, drivers can help to make the roads of California safer for everyone.

In addition to the knowledge and skills required to pass the practice driving tests, it is also important for drivers to be aware of the various laws and regulations that apply to driving in California. These include laws related to speed limits, seat belt use, cell phone use, and other important safety measures. By following these laws and regulations, drivers can help to ensure their own safety and the safety of others on the road.

It is also important for drivers to be aware of the potential consequences of violating these laws and regulations. In California, driving under the influence of alcohol or drugs, speeding, and other traffic violations can result in fines, points on a driver's license, and even jail time. It is essential for drivers to understand the seriousness of these consequences and to do their best to avoid committing traffic violations.

In addition to the legal consequences of traffic violations, it is also important to consider the personal and societal costs of unsafe driving. Accidents and injuries resulting from reckless or negligent driving can have serious and lasting impacts on the lives of those involved, as well as their families and communities. By following all relevant laws and regulations, and by driving safely and responsibly at all times, drivers can help to reduce the risk of accidents and injuries on the road.

Overall, it is essential for all drivers in California to understand the importance of safe and responsible driving, and to do their part in helping to make the roads safer for everyone. By studying and preparing for the practice driving tests, and by following all applicable laws and regulations, drivers can help to ensure their own safety and the safety of others on the road.

Made in the USA
Las Vegas, NV
30 October 2023